Cowboy Spurs and Their Makers

Number Thirty-seven
The Centennial Series of the Association of Former Students
Texas A&M University

COWBOY SPURS
AND THEIR MAKERS

By Jane Pattie

Foreword by Don Worcester

Introduction by B. Byron Price

TEXAS A&M UNIVERSITY PRESS
College Station

The paper used in this book meets the minimum requirements of the
American National Standard for Permanence of Paper for Printed Library
Materials, Z39.48–1984. Binding materials have been chosen for durability.
∞

Library of Congress Cataloging-in-Publication Data
Pattie, Jane, 1935–
     Cowboy spurs and their makers / by Jane Pattie ; foreword by Don
Worcester ; introduction by B. Byron Price.—1st ed.
          p.   cm.—(The Centennial series of the Association of Former
     Students, Texas A&M University ; no. 37)
     Includes bibliographical references.
     ISBN 0-89096-343-6 (alk. paper);
     paper ISBN 0-89096-506-4 (alk. paper)
     1. Spurs—Southwest, New.   2. Spurs—Texas.   3. Blacksmiths—
Southwest, New—Biography.   4. Blacksmiths—Texas—Biography.
     I. Title.   II. Series.
     TT220.P37   1991
     739.4′779—dc20   90-10889
                                                                  CIP

To
P. M. Kelly
and the other artisans whose tools were
the forge and the anvil,
and to
Lloyd Mitchell and O. R. Huff,
who collected their spurs

Contents

Illustrations

Foreword

The cattle kingdom of the post–Civil War West—the era of Longhorn cattle and mustang cowponies, the open range, the long drives—gave the world an unforgettable folk hero, the cowboy. His basic needs were few—stock saddles, bits and spurs, hats and boots, shirts and pants. When the main period of the long drives began, cowboys used whatever was available: cavalry boots, remnants of Confederate uniforms, homespun shirts, Mexican saddles, bits, and spurs. In the next few decades, as local artisans and distant factories labored to meet the fast-growing demand, cowboy dress and gear became somewhat standardized. The names of certain makers or manufacturers became bunkhouse words—Levis, Justins, Stetsons, to name a few.

Bits and spurs, like boots and saddles, were mainly handmade in ranching centers. Cowboys were especially particular about saddles, boots, hats, and spurs and bought the best available. "Like ever'thing else he wore," Ramon Adams wrote in *The Old-Time Cowhand,* "the cowboy took a heep of pride in his spurs. Unless he was plumb down and out he wouldn't be caught wearin' a cheap, inferior pair, which he called 'tin bellies.'"

Blacksmiths generally started making spurs and bits as a favor to local cowboys. Those who were most skillful were usually swamped with orders, and what started as a sideline became their main activity. Like a number of the boot and saddle makers, several spur men became regionally famous. Most of them copied popular styles, such as the OK and gal-leg spurs. When saddle and harness companies began a mail-order business, the names of a few spur makers—Crockett, Kelly, Buermann, and others—became known on every western range.

Spur makers were individualistic craftsmen, developing their own stylistic trademarks. Locally or regionally famous during their active careers, many are remembered today only by spur collectors who admire their skill but know little of their lives. Fortunately, Jane Pattie, western writer and Quarter Horse raiser, began collecting information and interviewing old-time spur makers and their immediate descendants or former employees twenty years ago while Kelly and several others were still living. Otherwise, much of the history and lore of their craft would have been lost forever.

In this engaging account of the lives and works of the great spur makers and their techniques, Jane Pattie traces the craft from Mexico to the American West of the nineteenth and twentieth centuries. Students of western socioeconomic history, western history buffs, and spur collectors are indebted to her for preserving the stories of these little known artisans and their craft.

Don Worcester

Preface

These brief biographies of master craftsmen at the forge are not intended to be the final word on cowboy spur makers, but rather a beginning. Only in the last few years have aficionados become serious about collecting spurs made by these artisans, as well as interested in knowing about the men themselves. Unfortunately, we waited until almost too late to learn the whole story, for most of the old-timers are gone, and most of their records have disappeared. Of the blacksmiths who occasionally made spurs in the earlier years, nothing is known.

My own interest in spur makers began when I started collecting spurs as a teenager. Several years later I met Lloyd Mitchell of Gatesville, and O. R. Huff of Fort Worth, spur collectors who generously shared their vast knowledge of spurs and spur makers as well as their valuable collections. The three of us decided that the story of the cowboy spur makers should be written, and that I was the one to write it. Many of their spurs illustrate this book. (I myself took all the photographs not otherwise credited in the book, including the color pictures.) With their help and encouragement, I began a search for information, which I found in magazine and newspaper articles and in brief references in books about the West, but there was no one work devoted to the master craftsmen themselves.

I was indeed fortunate that several of the men who are the subjects of this book were still living and willing to tell their own stories. Now, when the volume is finally completed, sad to say, every one of them has died, including O. R. Huff, collector and himself a spur maker, who was such a valuable contributor.

Although the old-time spur makers are gone, a few men still emulate them, among them Jerry Lindley of Weatherford, Texas. To illustrate the art of making spurs, he graciously opened his shop to my camera and answered many questions as he shaped pieces of a Model A axle into spurs in much the same way it has been done for centuries.

This book is the product of many people's contributions. It is my hope that it will answer some questions and that it will stimulate even more.

For their time and knowledge and generous help, I wish to thank the following:

The late Eugene Chase, of Council Grove, Kansas, and his wife, my cousin, Tate Chase, who entertained me as a teenager at their Flint Hills ranch in the summers, when heaven was a horse and a saddle and stirrup-deep bluestem. Gene was a man who had lived with horses and cattle and the land. Hanging in his barn were old spurs, discarded singles, which he gave to me. They became treasured possessions, and they started me to wonder why a spur would have an anchor or a star stamped on it. That was the beginning of my collection of spurs.

My father and mother, Robert and Juanita Rogers, who loved Texas and their Western heritage and always encouraged my quest for knowledge.

My husband, Lyle, who heard the same jingle of spurs that I did and prowled the antique stores and big-ranch country with me in order to add to our collection. He has spent many a silent evening while I memorized spur catalogs and sat before my typewriter.

The noted historian and author Don Worcester of Aledo, Texas, my friend and mentor, who gave me constant encouragement and whose suggestions and editing improved my manuscript immeasurably.

The late Mitchell A. Wilder, director of the Amon Carter Museum of Western Art in Fort Worth, who recognized cowboy spur making as Western art and encouraged me to write this book, and Ron Tyler, formerly the museum's eminent historian, who generously gave his help.

Bo Cantrell, my neighbor, who shared his thoughts on spur collecting.

Jerry Lindley of Weatherford, who fired up his forge and shaped the hot steel for my camera to record.

Gaines deGrafenried of the Texas Ranger Hall of Fame, Waco, collector of spurs, pistols, saddles, and many things Western.

The late Pascal M. Kelly and his wife, Hettie Kelly, whose vivid memories spanned the years of the prominent cowboy spur makers, and their family, whose hospitality was truly Western. Mr. Kelly's mind was a storehouse of information concerning his business and all aspects of the trade. Those facts were the basis for not only the chapter on him but also much of the rest of this book.

Mrs. Burton L. (Dessie) Hanbury, director of the Dallam-Hartley Historical Association and sponsor of the XIT Museum, Dalhart, Texas, for her help and remembrances of her friendship with the Kellys while they lived in Dalhart.

Jack Thomas of Fallbrook, California, author, collector, and saddle maker, who opened his files and freely discussed the results of his research on cowboy and buckaroo spur makers.

The late Dr. Tom Reagan of Beeville, Texas, for a memorable day talking spurs, and Nancy Reagan for her patience while he and I pursued our interests and savored his collection of antique spurs "par excellence" until the wee small hours. Dr. Reagan was also an authority on the spurs of Joe Bianchi and other South Texas makers and generously shared the results of his study.

Ralph Emerson, Jr., of Newington, Connecticut, the most knowledgeable person I know concerning August Buermann and North & Judd, Eastern spur makers who gave the Westerners a run for their money. Ralph made his collection of all forms of spur memorabilia available, and his knowledge is the foundation of the chapters on the Eastern firms. He also directed me to Shirley Muter of North & Judd Manufacturing Company, Middletown, Connecticut, whose interest and sense of history give this modern-day corporation a tie to the good things of yesterday.

Monas Buermann Doyle of Brooklyn, New York, a woman who has inherited the drive and initiative of the Buermanns.

Diana McCain, assistant librarian of the Connecticut Historical Society, for her research into the Norths and the Judds of Connecticut, and Barbara S. Irwin, reference librarian for the New Jersey Historical Society, for her information concerning August Buermann.

James Stewart Osbourn, senior reference librarian, and Maizy L. Wedderburn, reference librarian, both of the New Jersey Reference Division of the Newark Public Library, Newark, New Jersey, who provided photographs and newspaper copies for the August Buermann chapter.

Many who contributed to the McChesney chapter: Mrs. Robert McChesney of Ardmore, Oklahoma, who shared her reminiscences; Enid Justin of Nocona, Texas, friend of the McChesneys and last manufacturer of the McChesney bits and spurs; Lewis W. Browning of Angleton, Texas, whose father, N. C. Browning, added to the McChesney fame with his artistry; Kirby McPherson of Santa Fe, New Mexico, and Clinton McPherson of Valley View, Texas, who grew up with the McChesney brood and contributed much to the chapter on the Gainesville spur maker; Dean Foster, of the McCurtain County (Oklahoma) Historical Society; Adrienne Grimmett, librarian of Pauls Valley, Oklahoma, who put me in touch with people in the know; Joe Willard, of Pauls Valley, whose memory of the McChesneys and of his hours of making McChesney spurs there added greatly to the account; Eva Wall of Pauls Valley, who spent time and money on my research and made available to me the friendship and help that I would otherwise have missed from several others—Van Sparks, Virgie Castro, Jewell Panell, Stella Wall, and Edna (Mrs. Tom) McChesney, all of Pauls Valley.

My special thanks to Joe Bowman of Houston, a square shooter both as an individual and with pistols and a rifle, and to his friend and mine, Bob Taylor of Santa Fe, who made available to me his hospitality and his beautiful collection of spurs and catalogs from many makers and dealers, as well as his extensive research on the Bianchis of Victoria, Texas.

Lt. Col. Charles Schad (Ret.) of Gainesville, Texas, who shared his photographs and recalled his grandfather, G. A. Bischoff.

Charles P. Shipley II of Prairie Village, Kansas, for background on the noted Shipley family and the Charles P. Shipley Saddlery and Mercantile Company, for years the cattlemen's meeting place in Kansas City.

Mrs. Oscar Crockett of Boulder, Colorado, for her recollections of the good years in Kansas and Colorado, and Al Gabriella of Boulder, who had worked for Oscar and continued the Crockett tradition for Crockett, Renalde & Kelly.

Mary Causey Anglin and her son and daughter-in-law, Mr. and Mrs. Robert Causey Anglin, all of Safford, Arizona, who answered many questions concerning the life and craft of the noted Bob Causey. A special thanks to my sister-in-law, Jo Rogers of Scottsdale, who did double duty as secretary and chauffeur in Arizona. And to Lee Hubbard, director of the City Museum of Carlsbad (New Mexico), who made available the museum's Causey spurs.

The late Bob, Pate, and Dee Boone, Westerners to the core, each of whom added the facts of his own colorful life to the Boone chapter, and Blanche Gollager of San Diego, California, Bob's daughter, who shared her family photographs and information.

Jeannie Castello, reference librarian at Tom Green County Library in San Angelo, for her Boone research; Marisue Potts of Floydada for sharing her knowledge of Wallie Boone's business in Motley County; and Jack Fuqua of Amarillo, who verified and added information concerning his father's continuation of Wallie Boone's business for its brief time in Amarillo.

J. O. Bass, Jr., of Plainview, Texas, who graciously granted a telephone interview concerning his father during his years of shaping hot steel into works of art, and Billie Sue Gayler of the Swisher County museum, who furnished photos of Bass and of the replica of his shop.

The late Ed Blanchard of Yucca, Arizona, who recalled his past and opened his shop to me, and Mrs. Arthur H. Blanchard of Cherry Valley, California, who added to the final chapter of Ed's life.

The late Adolph Bayers of Truscott, Texas, whose dry wit gave a little burr to a smooth afternoon of talking spur-making methods and recalling the years that changed a cotton picker to an artisan, and Fannie Lois Bayers, who added the finishing touches to the Bayers story, and photographer Bank Langmore for use of his image of the noted spur maker.

John Treadwell of Fort McKavett, Texas; Mrs. Lawrence "Blackie" Williamson, Louie Lehne, and the late Frances Fish, all of Menard, Texas; Juanita Buntyn of Sonora, Texas; and Ruby Wagoner of the Menard Historical Museum, all of whom generously shared their memories of the illusive Jess Hodge; and especially Lynell Wheless of Menard, who put me in touch with these helpful people and with rancher Jack Baker of Sonora, a collector of Jess Hodge spurs.

Wayne Spiller of Voca, Texas, who researched the newspapers and files in search of answers to the Jess Hodge question.

The late Arthur Woodward of Patagonia, Arizona, a brilliant man who always had time to teach and was rarely at a loss for an answer.

Myrene Law of Smithfield, Texas, who has tirelessly typed and retyped and made my scribbled pages into an orderly, clean manuscript.

James Wheat of Mentone, Texas, whose hospitality made it possible for me to enjoy and photograph his numerous spurs, many of which are now at Texas Tech University's Ranching Heritage Center, and Rick Willeford, who made me aware of Jim's exceptional collection.

My special thanks to Dwight Huber of Canyon, Texas, collector, historian, photographer, author, and publisher of the *Spur Collectors' Quarterly* and *Western Collectibles Quarterly,* who opened his home and his wide scope of information to me. His knowledge not only of the evolution of Spanish Colonial–Mexican espuelas to cowboy spurs, but also of the work of J. O. Bass and many other makers is reflected throughout this volume. His spur collection equaled the best.

And I am doubly indebted to Byron Price, former director of the Panhandle-Plains Historical Museum, Canyon, Texas, and his staff there, particularly Norman Stewart, who assisted in my search through the museum's collection of spurs and equipment, including Adolph Bayers's dies, stamps, and records, plus file cabinets full of catalogs of makers and their jobbers and dealers.

And to Byron Price in his present role as executive director of the National Cowboy Hall of Fame and Western Heritage Center, Oklahoma City, for his help and participation in this book and for making available the museum's historical papers, photographs, and separations for the color plates; and to his staff there, particularly Marcia Preston, editor of *Persimmon Hill,* and Richard Rattenbury, the very able curator of history.

Without the availability of the knowledge and extensive collections of Lloyd Mitchell and O. R. Huff and the help of Lloyd's family and his wife, Madge, and Mayme Huff Thompson, who has always taken an active interest in her father's spur collection, this book would never have been begun or, years later, completed. Their forbearance is appreciated and their friendship valued.

Many people are responsible for this book—those mentioned above and many not listed. To all I say, "Thank you!" It is my hope that this is the beginning. There is more to tell.

—Jane Pattie

Cowboy Spurs and Their Makers

Introduction:
History of the Cowboy Spur

by B. Byron Price

The vaqueros who accompanied Spanish cattle herds into the Southwest beginning in the late seventeenth century rode with fierce-looking spurs that emitted a strangely soothing, musical sound and bore the majestic appellation *espuela grande*. A direct descendant of styles developed in Europe during the Middle Ages, this "great spur" of the conquistadors sired offspring that have served mounted warriors and nomadic herders for more than four centuries.

Spurs provide riders with a simple means of motivating, signaling, and controling their mounts while freeing the hands to perform other tasks. Beyond their basic function, however, the design, construction, and ornamentation of spurs reflect such complex and diverse factors as personality, fashion, and mechanization. Moreover, spurs embody mythic, romantic, and symbolic qualities that help bind horsemen into a legendary fraternity. Among cowboys, few items of attire are more distinctive and no element of gear save the stock saddle more celebrated than spurs.

Spurs have been recovered from Greek and Middle Eastern tombs, dating perhaps as early as 700 B.C. The evolution of mounted warfare through the centuries affected spur design, and over time spurs also became a status symbol. In Georgian England spurs were worn nearly everywhere—even to church, where the ringing of rowels became so prevalent and disruptive that the clergy fined offenders.

Cortés introduced the *espuela grande*—with its drooping shanks, narrow heel bands, and huge rowels between six and ten inches in diameter—from Spain to the New World in 1520. Spur-making blacksmiths, who often doubled as armorers, appeared on the upper Rio Grande as early as 1598. During the two centuries that followed, a constant demand for weapons, tools, and riding gear for Borderlands outposts from Texas to California kept smiths busy at their forges despite a recurring scarcity of imported bar iron.

Although the popularity of large rowels lasted less than one hundred years in Europe, the style persisted much longer in New Spain. Along the Spanish Borderlands, conquistador-type spurs were still handed down from one generation to the next long after they had passed from prominence in the more settled regions of Mexico.

Nevertheless, a second-generation Spanish colonial spur eventually developed and was popular between the mid-sixteenth and early nineteenth centuries. The traditional six- or eight-pointed rowels diminished in size and were eventually replaced by wheels with serrated edges, engraving, or openwork. The shanks also became shorter.

During the 1600s spurs inlaid with silver, brass, and sometimes gold or semiprecious stones had begun to appear among Spanish *ricos*. The artistic impulses of master smiths were translated into elaborate decorations through such tedious processes as engraving, chasing, damascening, and piercing. Some artisans even cast and hallmarked a few solid silver spurs.

The easily broken, scrolled shank decorations of conquistador models gave way to a crest known as an *intermedio*, later called a chap guard or buck hook, which was sometimes shaped like a flower or an animal. Moorish influence gave Spanish spurs decorative details such as the pomegranate-flower rowel pin often erroneously called a squash blossom. Geometric and floral forms abounded as ornamental motifs.

For most Spanish herders and soldiers, however, decorative spurs proved the exception rather than the rule, particularly in the sparsely populated Borderlands region. Scarce raw materials and rugged frontier conditions begot mostly plain, crudely fashioned gaffs only vaguely imitative of their more ornate counterparts farther south.

With the decline of the Spanish empire during the early nineteenth century, there developed yet another distinctive New World spur. Somewhat heavier and generally less ornamented than before, the new type possessed a shorter shank and smaller rowels, compared by one European observer to "five shilling pieces, generally divided into five blunt prongs shaped like a star. . . . [which] bruise a horse and hurt him excessively though they rarely puncture the skin."[1]

The relatively short-lived era of these transitional models ushered in the classic period in Mexican spur making that extended from the 1860s into the early twentieth century. Ornate silver inlay in Grecian key and geometric motifs, swinging buttons and shanks shaped usually as figure-eights or coiled snakes characterized the heavy *espuela Mexicana*. The finest examples of these spurs originated in the mining districts of central Mexico surrounding Amazoc, Guadalajara, and Zacatecas, but traders bound for the American Southwest acquired them by the hundreds at the trade fairs in Chihuahua, and before long cowboys north of the Rio Grande were calling them Chihuahuas.

Cowpunchers, drovers, and rangers of the Southwest particularly favored Mexican spurs equipped with *pajados*—danglers, clinkers, or jingle bobs. Suspended from the rowel pin, these pear-shaped metal pendants provided a distinctive musical accompaniment for a cowboy, whether mounted or on foot. During the early 1850s, a traveler in Mexico described a vaquero "armed with the huge Spanish spur, to which is attached a small ball of finely-tempered steel, that strikes against the long rowels at every tread of the man or beast and rings like a fairy bell. . . ."[2] Little wonder that Texas cowboys of the 1870s and 1880s christened such types "bell spurs."[3]

Jingle bobs helped lighten the monotony and loneliness of open-range work for both horse and rider. In town, they performed a distinctly social function. Ella Bird Dumont remembered that, when she was a young bride on the northwestern Texas frontier during the late 1870s, "very few of the cowboys were married, and when a woman was met, there was much bowing, scraping, and rattling of boots and spurs."[4] In some sections visiting cowboys routinely slipped their spur leathers into the "town notch," loosening them so that the rowels would ring off the boardwalks. Drop shanks achieved similar effects, as did heel chains when disconnected and allowed to drag.

In 1891 journalist Edgar Rye reported from Fort Griffin, Texas, that

> The large Mexican spurs that dangle from the cowboy's heels. . . . when successfully manipulated by a full-fledged cowboy along the pavement of cities and towns are capable of making as much noise as a hand-organ in full blast. The fashions in spurs has [sic] changed in latter years. The old three-inch rowel, that rolled along with a sound like the buzzing of machinery in a large factory, has given way to a smaller sized and much neater pattern that has a musical sound, like the tinkling of a small bell. Next to his six-shooter the cowboy considers his spurs a necessary appendage in his "make-up", and will not part with them even at dances and social gatherings.[5]

Isolation and distance from sources of supply bedeviled herders intent on equipping themselves with a serviceable pair of spurs. Those without access to local bit and spur markets depended on the meager stock of local merchants or special orders to fill their needs. In most cases cowboys' pocketbooks were smaller than their dreams. As a boy living in the Texas Hill Country, R. H. Crosby had eyed a pair of spurs among the merchandise of a peddler's wagon and had collected a two-hundred-pound barrel of the "finest pecans you ever saw gathered on the Perdinales [sic] River," in hopes of trading for them. Driving a hard bargain, the trader bartered the future cowman only one spur for the pecans and required him to fill a second barrel to secure the mate several months later.[6]

In most locales unornamented, utilitarian styles could be acquired for less than a dollar. The mass-produced types manufactured by such major eastern suppliers as the August Buermann Company of Newark, New Jersey, regularly found their way into cow camps throughout the western United States. Buermann stamped one of his most inexpensive offerings with the letters "O.K." and sold thousands of them to cowboys before custom-made spurs became the mark of a good hand. Thereafter, cheaply made spurs like the O.K. lost their respectability and became associated with inexperience or bad luck.

The advent of corporate ranching following the Civil War further influenced western spur styles and use. Outfits financed with eastern and foreign capital typically forbade employees to own personal livestock, providing them instead with a string of company-owned mounts. Insisting on the humane treatment of their remudas, management frowned upon sharp-roweled spurs. Prudent cowpunchers, therefore, filed the points off their rowels or chose large rowels with a great number of points because they were less harsh. Some punchers, preferring quirts in thorny, mesquite-infested regions, disdained spurs altogether, believing they confused and upset well-trained cowhorses. With or without the promptings of corporate policy, good hands did not employ their spurs as instruments of abuse. They generally avoided spurs with locking rowels, which easily lacerated or even pierced a horse's hide.[7]

Sometimes the alteration of spurs went beyond the blunting of rowels. Cowboys frequently replaced worn or harsh rowels altogether. Smooth iron washers provided a simple but effective substitute, as did decorative Mexican silver pesos. Many cowboys also modified the buttons, decorative ornament, and even the shank shapes of their spurs to suit their needs.

By the 1880s cowboy spurs in Texas and on the Great Plains began to show somewhat more adornment. While the proliferation of relatively inexpensive yet ornamental Mexican models accounted for at least part of the change, the influence of California-style spurs cannot be denied.

Judging from their memoirs, many trail drivers apparently gave up their unadorned, utilitarian models for the silver-garnished California types available from merchants and saddleries at many Northern Plains trail termini. Cowboys arriving in Texas from regions farther west sometimes brought with them styles created in places like San Jose and Santa Clara. Charlie Siringo told of one such California-trained range boss who persuaded many of the LX Ranch hands in the Texas Panhandle to order saddles, spurs, bits, and rawhide riatas from the West Coast. A few years later another Panhandle outfit encountered the Colorado-based Cross L cowboys of the Prairie Land and Cattle Company. According to Texan Harry Ingerton, the Cross L hands had "beautiful saddles, and they [had] these sixty foot ropes, rawhide ropes, and twenty-five dollar bits and spurs, silver mounted, and conchos as big as your hand on each side, and the most beautiful horses...." Feeling impoverished by comparison, Ingerton recalled, "Right then I decided I'd quit the T Anchors. That was too sorry an outfit for me."[8]

Toward the end of the nineteenth century, however, Texas blacksmiths began to produce their own distinctive style, which eventually eclipsed the popularity of Mexican, California, and eastern models among the herders of the Southwest and the Southern Plains.

Spur makers usually numbered or named their most popular styles for easy reference. Those who specialized in custom work frequently operated from drawings and specifications brought or sent in by their customers. The most productive and successful artisans usually offered cowboys a choice of spur sizes, weights, and qualities. In addition, customers usually picked rowel shape and button type as well as shank and heel-band style and dimensions.

Shank length and cant, whether raised, straight, or drooping, depended largely on the physical characteristics of a horseman and his mount. A long-legged rider with a small horse, for example, normally required spurs with a long or raised shank, while shorter riders, whose feet hung closer to their horses' flanks, frequently sought short-shanked drooping types.

Whatever the design, durability characterized spurs worn on the western ranges. Besides bar stock, resourceful frontier blacksmiths forged their creations from an incredible array of materials, including wagon, buggy, and automobile springs and axles, mowing machine blades, and harrow teeth. One blacksmith in Dripping Springs, Texas, even fashioned a useful pair of spurs from the middle tines of a pair of pitchforks. The proud owner pronounced them the best pair he had ever owned.

Companies that mass-produced spurs utilized various grades of metal ranging from the cheapest malleable iron to bar stock or steel plate. So-called non-rust alloys marketed by Buermann and his successors under such trade names as Star Steel Silver and Hercules Bronze also proved serviceable. From the late 1930s until after World War II, lightweight bits and spurs made from cast or extruded aluminum known as "airplane metal" enjoyed brief popularity, though the metal did not lend itself to ornamental mountings.

Finishes varied from region to region. Texas and southwestern cowboys favored the natural look of gray iron, which aged and rusted to a pleasing patina. Some even buried their new spurs for awhile to hasten the process. California spur makers, on the other hand, highlighted the bright silver inlay of their creations by bluing the spur body. Later makers plated some of their products with nickel and chrome.

Most "silver-mounted" spurs and bits actually were decorated with ornaments made of German or nickel silver, sometimes called white brass. Southwestern makers also soldered decorative pieces of copper, bronze, and brass to the surface of their spurs. Partly because of the nature of these metals, engraving was minimal, usually only a few cuts in a simple geometric, border, or wheat pattern. A few Texas makers experienced in working with pure silver embellished their creations with more extravagant and heavily engraved inlay work. Most, however, avoided the time and expense of inlay, confining their silver work to overlaid coin-covered buttons, rowel pins, and heel bands.

A vast array of individual decorative elements adorned cowboy spurs . They ranged from simple geometric patterns crudely punched or engraved in the spur body to fine mountings and inlay in a multitude of ornamental shapes. Indicative of one of the cowboys' favorite pastimes, symbols from playing cards commonly appeared as a motif on spurs. Among Texans, star-shaped mountings and rowels never failed to please. Often referred to as the "Texas Star," the device appeared with such regularity on saddles, chaps, and boots that Philip Ashton Rollins observed in his classic work on the cowboy, "the manufacturers . . . starred the equipment of almost everybody who did not object."[9]

Precious stones also occasionally appeared on spurs. R. L. Causey once made a pair with ruby-inlaid heel bands for steer-roping champion Clay McGonagill, and a craftsman with time on his hands at Huntsville Prison experimented with abalone mountings. At eighteen dollars, the most expensive of the twenty-two Kelly Brothers styles illustrated in an early twentieth-century trade catalog possessed pearl-mounted heel bands. It is unlikely, however, that many jewel-bedecked creations ever made it to the range. Ostentatious creations like J. R. McChesney's peacock spur and bit set, available with rhinestones, rubies, and emeralds set in the tail feathers, probably were restricted to parade or festive wear by recreational riders and showmen.

As spur artistry became more complex, the desire for fresh designs led to a revival of such exotic natural forms as birds, snakes, and animals. While makers concentrated most of the mounting and inlay work on heel bands, the shanks and rowels also contributed decorative lines. Under the touch of a skilled craftsman, a spur shank might be transformed into the graceful sway of a goose neck or the shapely form of a woman's stockinged leg.

The aesthetic sense of makers notwithstanding, few forces influenced the ornamentation of spurs more than show business. Wild West shows, and later motion pictures, television, and rodeo all helped create and sustain a mythic cowboy hero identified in part by his dress and the tools of his trade. The colorfully garbed participants in Buffalo Bill's Wild West Show and its imitators created a lasting public image of the rough riders who dominated the cattleman's frontier. Some of the cowboys-turned-showmen performed with flashy bits and spurs decorated with Indian-, horse-, and buffalo-head ornaments, which Cody himself is said to have had a hand in designing. Thanks to the skillful promotion of eastern makers, such flamboyant models eventually reached horsemen around the world.

As the popularity of Wild West extravaganzas ebbed, screen actors transferred the spectacle of cowboy life to motion pictures. Many of the early silent western films featured genuine cowboys fresh from the range. Ex-punchers intent on impressing directors and casting agents began replacing their authentic gear with fancier outfits, which included tall-crown, wide-brim hats, wool-covered chaps, and gaudy silver-encrusted saddles, bits, and spurs.

Sensing a lucrative market for high-quality saddlery among the wealthy southern California clientele, Swedish-born Edward H. Bohlin opened a shop that specialized in elaborate saddles, bits, and spurs ornamented in the California tradition. Bohlin, who had worked as a cowhand in Montana and later as a trick rider and roper before migrating to Hollywood, fashioned spurs for many movie greats, including cowboy-turned-actor Tom Mix. This top-of-the-line model sold for $650 and featured sterling silver overlay accented with gold scroll and flower designs, rope trim, and rowel pin heads.

Promoters awarded trophy spurs crafted by Bohlin and other makers to contestants at rodeos throughout the West. Rodeo performers represented a specialized market for western spur makers. The special rules and requirements of the sport and the desire for competitive advantage led in one case to the development of a more efficient bronc-riding spur with a drop shank and blunt rowel that facilitated the movement of a rider's legs as he "scored" his bucking mount.

More than one enterprising spur maker associated his products with legendary rodeo performers and cowboy actors in an effort to increase sales. Famous places also made for memorable names. Texan Wallie Boone, for example, charged $360 for his diamond-studded Madison Square Spur and offered the sterling silver Hollywood Special for $50. Alluring tags such as Diamond Dick, Bronco Buster Special, Arizona Bill, Miles City Special, The Alamo, The Vaquero, and The Plainsman typified early approaches to spur marketing.

A few of the most prominent makers reached customers through mail order catalogs, leaflets, and advertising cards. Newspapers and stockmen's magazines such as the *Cattleman* also heralded the work of the important artisans. Most craftsmen could not afford to advertise and relied upon word of mouth or some innovative method of making their work known. Bob Causey, for example, displayed examples of his bits and spurs in a saloon in Eddy, New Mexico, where he successfully raffled off a matched pair each Saturday night when the place was full of eager cowboys and ranchers. At his San Angelo shop, Wallie Boone drew attention to his products by creating and exhibiting the world's largest steel spur, measuring sixteen feet long and weighing four hundred pounds.

Only the largest and best-known makers effectively competed beyond their locality or region. For these giants of the trade, the shops and catalogs of western saddlemakers and clothing manufacturers offered one of the most important outlets. A catalog produced by the Schoellkopf Company of Dallas during the 1920s, for example, carried twenty-two styles of Kelly Brothers, fourteen of McChesney, and thirty of the eastern-based North & Judd Company. A Padgitt Brothers saddlery catalog of somewhat earlier vintage carried thirty-nine styles of Buermann, twenty-seven varieties of Kelly Brothers, and twenty-eight types of McChesney.

Surprisingly, relatively few makers marked their products. Those who did usually placed their name and perhaps a style or sequential number inside the heel band or under the button. Others identified their creations with such simple trademarks as the North & Judd anchor or August Buermann's star. Most spur makers, however, depended upon distinctive design and workmanship to distinguish their products from those of their competitors.

Nearly all guaranteed their products against defects. One-piece, heavy-duty, Texas-style spurs gained a well-deserved reputation for durability, although lost rowels and mountings often required replacement. Even makers who specialized in ornamental models for recreational riders took fierce pride in the quality of their spurs. "We have not lost sight of the boys who still ride the range," Edward Bohlin wrote in a 1930s catalog, "and their needs for serviceable rigging that will 'stand the gaff.'"[10]

Because few records of spur shops survive, it is difficult to determine what volume an individual craftsman produced. Depending on the amount and intricacy of decoration and the extent to which power tools and specialized mechanics were employed, a pair of spurs could take a week or more to make; most took only a day or two. One highly mechanized shop claimed to have produced more than twenty thousand pairs during one six-year period.[11]

Whatever their output, spur makers usually produced other goods as well. Typical frontier blacksmiths fashioned everything from branding irons to farm implements. Besides his regular bit and spur business, one Texas maker took time out to forge a steel fence to surround the local city hall, while another of his colleagues invented and held an early patent for a squeeze cattle chute. Most made other riding hardware like cinch rings and bits, and later some product lines specialized in such items as dehorners and stock trailers. Bohlin's atypical offerings even included Spanish iron work for furniture decoration and ornamented dog collars, traveling bags, make-up cases, and pocket books.

Still other talented craftsmen combined their spur making with additional occupations. Some were cowboys but most were mechanics or blacksmiths; a few used their talents in such related pursuits as painting and cabinetry. The daughter of Adolph Bayers, an important twentieth-century Texas spur maker whose primary vocation was farming, believed that tending the soil preserved her father's "purity from mechanization or automation. He resisted anything that might compromise the quality of his product. If he had been dependent on spur making for a living, I think he might have somehow felt compelled to make some compromises in the interest of quantity and speed." [12]

The painstaking effort and perfectionist tendencies that characterized the one-man spur shops often caused them to fall behind in their orders by months or even years. Whether they were caught up or not, the arduous road to fame rarely led to fortune. A desire to keep their products reasonably priced in the face of continually rising labor and material costs prompted progressive spur makers to mechanize at least part of their operations. A few, intent on stepping up output, created dies adapted to mass production and employed specialists to perform such operations as forging, grinding, polishing, mounting, and engraving. The cost of developing expensive dies and maintaining extensive inventories, however, created a financial burden that few could endure, and the lure of handmade quality kept many small-scale spur makers in business long after the dinosaurs of the industry had vanished.

Rapid communication and the influence of the media have gradually eroded the regional distinctiveness of spurs, though scores of new designs have been developed and put on the market. Local custom and tradition, however, die hard in the conservative ranch country where good hands are still judged in part by the quality of their gear. There was a time long passed when spurs, once strapped in place, became a permanent fixture on a cowman's boots. A few, like the celebrated ranchman and trail driver Ab Blocker, wore theirs to their graves.

Spurs still hold an honored place among western riders. As in bygone times, a good pair of spurs, like a valued hunting rifle or other precious family heirloom, often is passed from one generation to the next. And cowboys still part with them only under duress, usually with reluctance, and always with the hope that their new owner will "make a hand."

Part I

Spurs and Spur Making

Chapter 1

Spurs

The portion of Western history this book is intended to preserve was destined to become obsolete by the cranking of the first automobile. The old-time blacksmith became an endangered species, and the days when he shaped a red-hot spur to fit the heel of a cowboy boot have disappeared like the smoke from his forge. The spurs used by cowboys in Texas and elsewhere in the Southwest were more than tools of their trade. They were works of art—skillfully made items that showed the craftsmanship of their makers as well as their wearers' skill and sense of professionalism.

The men chosen as the subjects of these chapters were among the leaders in the field of making cowboy spurs. Their reputations as craftsmen spread throughout the great plains and wherever there were horsemen. Many of their contemporaries made spurs when they had the time or orders, but few of them made the quantity and quality or enjoyed the fame of the men featured here. Some marked their products and others did not, but many of the spurs were works of art.

Most spurs discussed in this book were made by independent spur makers or blacksmiths in small shops in the West, but two eastern firms mass-produced spurs and bits that were popular with cowboys for many years. The August Buermann Company in New Jersey and North & Judd Manufacturing Company in Connecticut filled many orders in the 1870s and later. They made a whole array of spurs, from European and military to all of the styles popular on the cattle ranges of the West. By around 1917 cowboys were changing from the file-finished type of spur to polished, better-made spurs. It was not long before the public and retail stores alike were buying the higher quality varieties, and many of the country blacksmiths were disappearing from the spur scene.

The "Big Three" in the spur business in the 1920s were J. R. McChesney, P. M. Kelly, and Oscar Crockett. McChesney had the market sewed up during the early 1900s, Crockett was going great guns from the 1920s through the 1940s, and Kelly was a major competitor of both companies. The three men had much in common. They all began as cow-country blacksmiths, and they knew how to shape a spur to fit a horseman's boot. As the demand for their products grew, they were willing to tool up for certain processes to save time as long as they could retain the hand-craftsmanship for which they were noted. They equipped their shops with punch presses, dies, and other machinery for producing spurs much faster. When many of the other spur makers were turning out excellent hand-crafted products in limited numbers, these three leaders expanded to meet larger markets without actually turning to mass production.

Cowboys proudly show off their spurs, 1903. *Photo by M. Sherman. Courtesy Denver Public Library, Western History Department.*

Three kinds of spurs have been most important to spur wearers of the Southwest: the Mexican spur, the California or buckaroo spur, and the Texas or cowboy spur.

The Mexican spur is the forerunner of the cowboy spur made by the early blacksmiths of Texas and the Southern Plains. This Mexican spur, as it commonly appeared during the first three-quarters of the nineteenth century, had flat heel bands and dropped shanks with only an indication of a crest or chap guard. The multispoked rowels were smaller than those of Spanish colonial days, and from their rowel pins dangled *pajados,* bits of iron that later American cowboys called jingle bobs.[1] Some of the early western spurs made by both North & Judd and the Buermann company appear to have been copied from this traditional style of Mexican spur or perhaps from the similar buckaroo spur.

The more ornate version of the Mexican spur that developed during the 1860s was the charro spur, known to later U.S. horseman as the Chihuahua spur. It typically had wide, sculptured, silver-inlaid heel bands with ornate swinging buttons. The large rowels had eight or more *espigas* or spokes, sometimes interlaced with filagree. Mexican spurs were always hand-forged and never cast. As silver inlay became popular, smiths panistakingly hammered silver into deep-cut grooves to ornately decorate the spurs and then treated the iron with a bluing process known as *pavón,* which had been developed in Amazoc de Mota, a spur-making center since the time of Cortés.[2]

Horse gear was taken to California from Mexico along with cattle and horses.

The Californios were of Spanish and Indian descent and remained in contact with Mexican culture longer and more closely than did the Texans. As a result, California spurs have more nearly retained the characteristics of their Mexican antecedents than have the cowboy spurs of Texas and the Southern Plains.

The California buckaroo (buckaroo is a corruption of the Spanish word *vaquero*) spur was generally of two-piece construction—the shank and the heel band. It was usually full-mounted, with silver inlay on both sides of the heel band and shank, engraved elaborately, and often blued. It typically had stationary buttons and double heel chains.[3]

Texas-sytle spurs were forged of one piece, in contrast, with either swinging buttons or stationary buttons, usually on turned-up heel bands. They were generally only half-mounted and featured overlaid decorations on the outside of the band. The hand-filed steel was not blued. These spurs did not have heel chains and rarely had chap guards. Cowboy spurs were generally plainer and more utilitarian than their California cousins.[4]

The spurs of the Northern Plains area were a combination of California and Texas styles. They were generally of one-piece construction and were decorated with either inlay or overlay, as well as silver conchas, which were often used on both shanks and heel bands. Many of these spurs were beautifully engraved and of fine work-

The Spur
and Its Parts

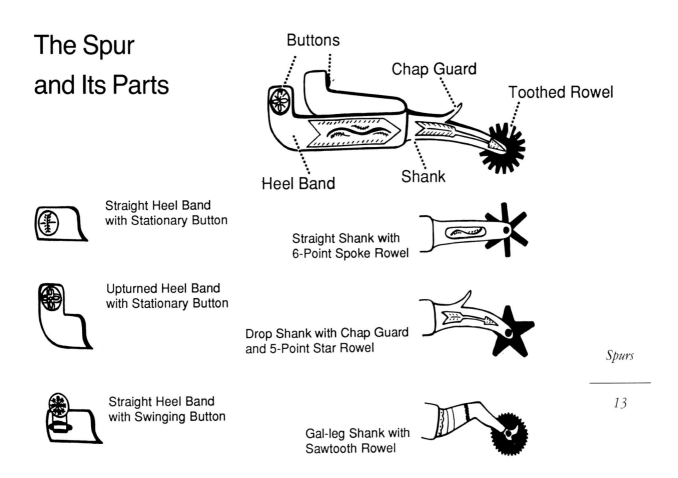

Spurs

manship. Some of the makers, especially artists such as Phillips and Gutierrez of Cheyenne, Wyoming, and Schnitger of Gillette, Wyoming, marked their spurs, but most did not identify their creations. Many of the saddle shops of the Northern Plains carried, in addition to locally made spurs, the Texas-style spurs made by McChesney in Texas and later Oklahoma, Kelly in Texas, or Crockett in Kansas and then Colorado, as well as those manufactured by the mass-production companies of North & Judd and Buermann in the East.[5]

The Texas spurs featured a variety of styles, many known by their shank design or ornamentation. The gal-leg and the gooseneck, for instance, featured shanks shaped and decorated to represent a woman's leg or a gracefully curved goose's neck, respectively. It is often impossible to trace the origin of a particular style.

There has been considerable speculation about who originated the popular gal-leg spur, for example. Some have credited McChesney and others R. L. Causey. One story has it that while McChesney was in Broken Arrow, Oklahoma, some cowboys from South Texas were in his shop, where the conversation soon got around to the women in the various cowtowns. It is said that this talk gave the blacksmith the idea of making the gal-leg spurs, for which he became famous. But the design might also have come to spurs originally from a gal-leg bit patented as design no. 17,040 (patent no. 220,322) by Frank M. Gilham of San Francisco, assignor to August Buermann. The application was filed on November 30, 1886, a year before McChesney began forging spurs and while Causey was involved mainly in general blacksmithing. The Buermann gal-leg bit was advertised in the 1898 Sears & Roebuck catalog and in the 1920s was still in the Buermann catalog in six styles.[6] No matter where the credit lies, there is no question that cowboys took to the style and many spur makers employed and profited from the gal-leg design. Soon many were making gal-legs with ther own variations.

There was a great deal of "borrowing" of designs among spur makers. Customers and drummers would bring sketches or examples of spurs they had seen and liked, and makers would see each other's wares in catalogs or store displays. Features might be combined in novel ways or variations on designs might distinguish a maker's work, but many of the essentials were copied. Moreover, spur makers sometimes bought spurs from other craftsmen when they had more orders than they could fill. It is possible to find, therefore, the same spur bearing different makers' names. P. M. Kelly, for example, told of selling his plain, unmarked spurs to García in California; García mounted and engraved them and sold them as his own.

Certain styles were popular in some parts of the country but would not sell at all in other areas. When a particular design was in demand, the various manufacturers apparently had few qualms about borrowing it. Some, like Kelly, would drop a style once it became a slow seller or when he added a new design. But others, like Buermann, who at one time had 450 styles listed in a single catalog, continued making and carrying all of their styles.[7]

There were two basic processes for making spurs, forging and casting. Forging was the more common of the two among the craftsmen in the small shops that dotted the West. Many of these spur makers were blacksmiths who also made other saddlery items and had all the equipment for forging at hand. Casting was done mostly by the large Eastern manufacturers who relied on quantity and the variety of their bit and spur lines, since theirs was a wholesale business, and they therefore needed to increase the volume of their sales.

Casting is done by pouring or injecting molten metal into a mold, where it hardens into the desired form. There are several casting processes, but one of the most common and widely used was sand casting, which could be used for all castable metals—bronze, brass, iron, steel, and a variety of proprietary brass and bronze alloys, such as Buermann's patented Hercules Bronze or North & Judd's similar Gun Metal. These brass and bronze alloys were corrosion resistant, of pleasing appearance, and with strength comparable to that of steel castings. They consisted mainly of a mixture of zinc, lead, tin, copper, and sometimes nickel, with phosphorus and other elements added.[8]

In sand casting, a pattern in the form of the piece to be cast is made of wood, or preferably metal, by the pattern maker from a drawing showing the dimensions and allowing for shrinkage. The pattern is placed in a wooden or metal box called a flask, and a special mixture of moist "green" sand and clay is packed firmly around the pattern to form the mold, which is made in two pieces to allow for the removal of the pattern. After the pattern is removed, the molten metal is poured through a gate into the cavity, and once the metal has hardened, the sand mold is broken away. When the casting has cooled, the excess metal from the gate is cut away, and the casting is tumbled to clean it before finishing. Sand casting is a simple process, but it requires an experienced foundry worker to obtain soundness in final castings. Castings are hard and brittle when they come from the mold; converting them to malleable iron requires an annealing process that involves heating and slow cooling under controlled conditions.[9]

Aluminum was also a popular metal for a time. The aluminum business did not originate with World War II, as some might think. A 1929 catalog featured the Martin Zephyr line of spurs made of "airplane metal." Aluminum spurs were extruded into special forms or in the case of bits, the cheek pieces were cut out with a saw. Spur collector Jack Thomas of Fallbrook, California, recalled being in the Martin shop in Los Angeles prior to 1936 and seeing that, even then, his spurs were made of this material. "I think that Martin was the originator of the idea of lightweight spurs," Thomas stated.

Another man who is touted as "one of the originators of the aitplane aluminum bit" was Ed Newhagen of the Ricardo Metals Manufacturing Company of Denver, a company that profited from the aluminum craze. Many of the spur makers tried it, but not many continued with it for long.

Although a few contemporary spur makers have clung to the old ways and continued to take pride in their handwork, for most, the time when the forge and the anvil were the principal tools has long since passed. Instead, they rely on stainless steel and acetylene torches. Many modern-day, machine-made spurs lack the vibrancy and that intangible handcrafted quality provided by the men whose sweat tempered the steel.

Ironically, the men who earned reputations as master craftsmen of handmade cowboy bits and spurs—P. M. Kelly, J. R. McChesney, Oscar Crockett, Bob Boone, Joe Bianchi, A. R. Bayers, R. L. Causey, and J. O. Bass—enjoyed their popularity after the days of the big cattle drives were over, near the turn of the century and later.

But cowboys on such Texas ranches as the 6666, the Triangle, and the Pitchfork still work cattle horseback. And even though the horse is no longer a necessity to people in other walks of life, the horse population has mushroomed and horse-oriented projects have become big business. Stetson hats and Levis are as likely to be found in Pennsylvania as in Texas, and like the old-time cowboy, today's rider wants spurs that are not only useful but distinctive. So even in this jet age, spur craftsmanship continues in great demand, not only among collectors but with men and women who are at home in the saddle.

Chapter 2

Visit with a Contemporary Spur Maker

The forge in the dim corner of the room glowed red as Jerry Lindley poked in it with his tongs, turning the piece of steel buried in the center of the coals, examining it for just the right color to indicate it was the proper temperature for hammering out, elongating, and shaping into the heel band of a spur. This was the first step in a process that has been followed for centuries by craftsmen around the world. Unlike his predecessors, Lindley, working in 1984 in Weatherford, Texas, was using a trip-hammer, electric-powered grinders and sanders, and a welding torch, which have replaced hammer work and muscle. His knowledge of metals and his methods of arriving at the finished product, however, were basically the same as those of spur makers throughout history.

Whether using muscle power or electricity, each artisan follows basically the same procedure in forging a pair of spurs. Lindley first cleaned the clinkers, or residue, from his forge so that the air from a blower could pass up through a fire box, which made it possible to control the heat. The fire was made inside an iron nest, which was about three-eighths of an inch thick, had fire brick around it, and was cemented over the top. Lindley placed wadded-up paper in the forge, crumbled coke (coal with the gases burned out) around the top of the paper, and set it afire. It caught easily and made a hot fire. He next packed coal around it, then raked the coals in as he needed them in order to keep the fire hot. The nest made it possible to have direct heat when needed, by concentrating the fire in one small area. He heated steel for both of a pair of spurs simultaneously. While he was working on one, the other was reaching the proper temperature for shaping. When one piece cooled, he put it back in the fire and worked on the other, so no time was lost.

"I use Model A axles and drive lines to make spurs," Lindley explained. "That steel can be hammered thin, because it's tempered and easily finished, which gives spurs a nice ring. The metal can be bent and shaped, and it will have spring, but it's not likely to break. Two axles will make five pairs of spurs. I cut the axle into pieces about 4¾ inches long. Each piece is split 2¾ inches down the center to make the heel bands, and depending on the style of spurs I'm making, I'll have 1½ to 2 inches left that's solid to form the shank."

Jerry heated the two pieces of axle and turned them in the coals until each was the right color to work. "When I first start beating the metal," he went on, "it's an

Jerry Lindley in his shop near Weatherford, Texas.

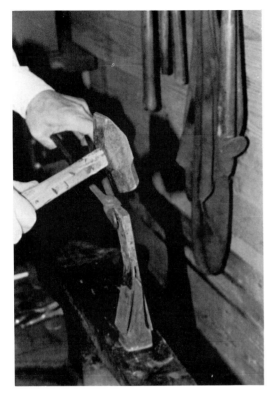 

It takes a piece of steel 4¾ inches long to make one spur. It is split down the center for 2¾ inches to make the heel band. Lindley spreads the two pieces to a T shape on his anvil.

The split steel is hammered out flat before it is shaped around a mold to form the heel shape.

Lindley heats the steel in a forge until it is the right color to work.

orange, just before being a straw color. That's the color I look for, depending on the amount of light in my shop. If the sunlight is coming in on the forge, you won't be able to see the colors of the iron when it melts. If you keep the room dark, you can tell when it's a cherry red or bright orange, and you'll know about what temperature it is."

"When the metal becomes this orange color where I can start beating it," Lindley continued, "it's soft and pliable. As it cools, it hardens and I have to reheat it. I use a trip-hammer to flatten the metal, but even if I were working on the anvil, it would need to be the same color. While the metal is heating in the forge, I'm always thinking about where I'm going to hit it. When it comes out of the forge, and I put it on the anvil or under the trip-hammer, I start working it immediately, because if I have to take the time to decide what I'm going to do, it will cool. The trip-hammer is faster, and it takes the place of a blacksmith's manual hammering, which is hard work. It would take two hours to hammer out a pair of spurs on the anvil.

"When the forging is flattened, it'll stretch and expand and is easily worked. If the spurs I'm making require a high shank, I'll spread the metal more before I stretch it. If the spur is to have a chap guard on the shank, I stretch the shank and then cut it with a chisel to turn the chap guard up. The chap guard isn't welded on. It's part of that shank." Lindley used the trip-hammer to beat the 1⅛-inch shaft until it was ½ inch thick and the arms that would form the heel band were from ¾ to 1 inch wide. The steel was approximately ⅛ inch thick when it was ready to be spread to form the heel band.

"I spread the arms flat until the forging is in the shape of a T," he explained. "If I'm going to do any work on the shank, I'll do it before I ever spread the arms, because once they're spread, there's no easy way to work it on the anvil."

Once the steel was in a T-shape and after any crack in the shank had been ground away, it was ready for the band to be bent into the proper shape to fit a boot heel. Jerry used a steel mold to get this shape. "I put the forging in my mold," he explained, "after it has been heated to an orange color, particularly around the shank and about two inches down the band on each side. That way I can hammer it to get the proper fold and make it even and smooth around the mold. The hotter it is, the easier it is to work. This is also the time to make sure that the spur is level."

The length of the band from the shank to the end was 4 inches at this time. The band of a finished spur is generally 3⅞ inches. A man with a large foot could wear a 4-inch band, and a smaller man or woman would wear a 3¾-inch band. The spur should be thicker where the heel band joins the shank, and it should gradually become thinner toward the buttons.

Lindley next worked the spur on the grinder and sander to remove the rough edges and smooth the band. If a small crack on the inside of the band had not been hammered out completely, the grinder removed it also. The inside was fairly smooth, because when the spur was beaten with the trip-hammer, the inside was on the solid part of the anvil. The outside became rough, because the trip-hammer left marks on the metal, and as the hot heel band was hammered around the mold, the outside of the band was roughed up. Lindley smoothed it with both the sander and a file. The sander is faster, but close places, like the bend of the knee and the calf of the leg on a gal-leg spur, require hand filing. Jerry used a three-cornered file to get to those areas.

A tin pattern with a finished spur made from it.

Lindley hand files the spokes of his rowels, which are made from blanks.

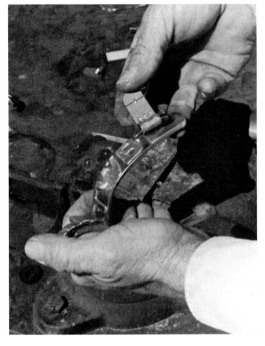

A button hinge is slipped onto a staple and closed.

Lindley evens the sides of the hinge in his vise.

The next step was to cut slots for the button hinges and mark the holes to be drilled for the staples or hinge pins and the rowel pins. Then he cut the slot in each shank for the rowels, and the rough edges were sanded smooth. "Before I put the hinge pins in for the swinging buttons, the whole spur will be tempered," Lindley explained. "That's the way I get my spurs to ring. I'll heat each spur in the forge and watch for the metal to reach a certain color. I look for colors; I really don't know the temperatures. When it reaches that point, I'll brush it off with a steel brush to get the slag off and drop it in a bucket of water. Then I'll sand it and clean it off. Next, I'll put in the staples for the swinging buttons."

He drills a 3/16-inch hole in each button hinge and countersinks it.

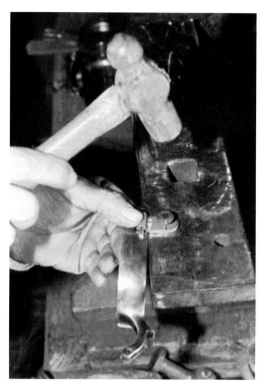

The button is hammered into the hinge cold.

The staples looked like fence staples, only flatter. The inside measurement from pin to pin was 7/8 inch. Lindley drilled two 3/16-inch holes from the outside of each side of each spur, countersunk them with a 1/4-inch bit, and bradded the staples in. There was no welding. They were hammered in cold, and they were there to stay. The pins to hold the rowels in the shanks were put in the same way.

Lindley made many of his tools and much of his equipment in the same way the old-time blacksmiths made theirs. His punch press was made from a clutch plate, a spline, and a pilot shaft. It was cut so that he could slide a piece of red-hot metal in it to punch out the rowels. Then he needed only to smooth them with a file. Usually, however, he marked his rowels on a steel disc, then cut them out and filed them by hand. "I collected old rowels for patterns," he said, "and I'll cut a disc out of a piece of 1/8-inch metal and smooth the edges to get it round. I mark with a waterproof pen where I want to cut the teeth, which I saw out by hand. I put the rowel disc in my vice and file the points. I want them all even and in line. Then I drill a hole through the center. When I'm through filing and drilling, I place a flat piece of metal over my forge in the fire and lay the rowels on it and let them heat until they reach a cherry red. Then I drop them in water to harden them."

Lindley's spurs were mounted mainly with silver and a little copper. He used a jeweler's saw to cut his mountings. When mounting a pair of gal-leg spurs, he first cut the shape of the leg out of silver for the stockings. Copper slippers and garters were cut out to complete the mounting for each shank, and a diamond, heart, club,

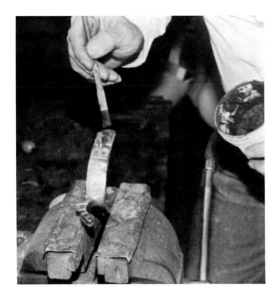

To make the silver overlay adhere to the steel, Lindley puts the spur in his vise and brushes the area and the mounting with silver solder.

The spur is heated with a torch to 1140° to seal the mounting with the melted solder, then dipped in water to cool the spur. The excess solder is then buffed off with a wire brush and a small file.

and spade might be placed on the outside of each heel band from the shank around to the button. To make sure the mountings on each spur matched perfectly, he put the two pieces together in a small vice and filed them until they were identical. The next step was to bend and shape each mounting to fit the curve of the heel band exactly. After that he put the spur in the vice and brushed the mounting and the spur with a flux, a silver solder. He set the mounting in place and held it with an ice pick while he heated the inside of the band of the spur with an acetylene torch. Flux is like a liquid paste; when it melted, it bonded the mounting to the spur.

"Silver solder melts at 1140 degrees, which is very hot," he said. "It seals the mounting on there. I've never been able to get a mounting off or a spur in one piece after using it. You could heat the lead solder like the old-timers used just a little and then slide the mounting off. In making a mate for a McChesney, for instance, when you put the lead solder on the mounting and on the spur and heated it, it would run and seal everything down. But then you'd have to go back and clean that excess off, and that's difficult. When you use the silver solder, all that shows is a little line right around the mounting. I can buff that off with a wire brush or just file it with a small file. When silver solder is put on correctly, you see no solder and there are no cracks under the mounting. It's sealed. You can't get that silver off unless you heat it red-hot, and then it'll only come off in pieces."

For making copper mountings, Lindley used .22-gauge sheets of copper or flattened copper tubing. Either can be engraved. He also buys silver in sheets. Lindley

Stamped LINDLEY and 21 under the inside swinging buttons on each spur. Half-mounted gal-leg spurs with copper shoes and garters and silver overlays for the stockings, the initials LBP on the heel band, a plate under the button and silver on the outside button. Engraved. *Pattie Collection.*

annealed the silver to soften it so he could be exact in cutting the shapes. In annealing a piece of silver, it is heated to a cherry red and dropped into water, which makes it soft and pliable rather than springy. It can then be rehardened by heating it again.

"When I make gal-leg spurs, if I use nickel silver for the stockings," Lindley continued, "I can anneal it and saw it out so I can shape it. Each leg is rounded, and I can shape the stocking to fit that curved leg. If it's not annealed, it's hard to mold it properly so it will fit."

To make the heart mountings for his stationary buttons, Lindley used a small tin heart-shaped pattern of the correct size and outlined the shape on the sheet of silver. He sawed out the silver heart and then soldered it onto the head of a wagon box rivet that served as a button. He drilled a ³⁄₁₆-inch hole in the spur band, then countersunk the button stud and bradded it down securely. According to Lindley, most of the old-time spur makers also used wagon box rivets for buttons. The head of that wagon box rivet was the backing for the silver heart mounting, and the sides of the head were ground down a little so they weren't wider than the heart. He poured silver solder onto the inside of the silver heart and onto the button, which he then heated with the torch so that the mounting bonded to the rivet.

"I find that one of the hardest things to do is put the copper and silver mountings next to each other where they fit smoothly," Lindley admitted. "For instance, if a heart is in the center overlapping a diamond on either side, I cut everything out and make them fit and bend each piece into shape. I solder the heart onto the band first and then slide each part of the diamond up to it. They not only have to match in size and shape, but fit in the same spot on each spur."

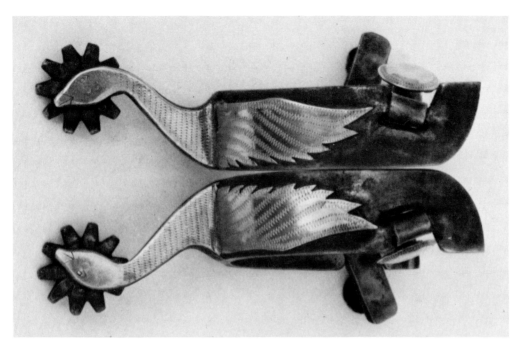

Stamped LINDLEY and spur number under the inside swinging button on each spur. Half-mounted goose-head spurs with the head and neck on the shank and the wing on the outside heel band, mounted with silver overlay and engraved. Swinging buttons are set at an angle. *Courtesy Jerry Lindley.*

After the mounting was on each spur, Lindley polished it, and it was ready for engraving. "Sometimes I draw a pattern," he said, "but most of the time, I just free-hand the design. If it looks good, I keep going. I use about twelve engraver's tools that I've made."

When the spurs were completed, he stamped LINDLEY and the number of the pair of spurs on each of them. If they had turned-up buttons, LINDLEY and the spur number were placed by the outside buttons. On spurs with swinging buttons, his name and number were on the outside button hinges. The steel stamp is harder than the spur, so he stamped his name on the spurs cold. "Each pair of spurs has both a pattern number and a serial number, so I can always go back in my records and look at the number of a pair of spurs and know whom I made them for, and I'll know everything I need to know to replace one if it's lost. I can duplicate any spur I've made, but, as with anything that's hand-made, no two pairs of spurs are just alike."

How long does it take to make a pair of spurs? "If I stay away from the coffee pot and don't have too many visitors," Lindley said, "I can make a pair of spurs with swinging buttons, mounted and engraved, in two days."

Spurs are the mark of the horseman, and a maker's stamp on a pair of spurs is the mark of the artisan.

Part II

Spur Makers

August Buermann in 1906. *Photo from* New Jersey: A Historical, Commercial and Industrial Review, *courtesy Newark Public Library, Newark, New Jersey.*

Chapter 3

August Buermann and His Star Brand Spurs

One of the most successful mass producers of spurs in the United States was the August Buermann Manufacturing Company of Newark, New Jersey. Buermann made every type of spur imaginable, and he was a master at distribution. His Star Brand spurs could be bought in saddle and harness shops from the Atlantic to the Pacific, in South America, Cuba, and Hawaii.[1] During the lifetime of his company, from 1868 until it was acquired by North & Judd Manufacturing Company of New Britain, Connecticut, in 1926, Buermann was both an innovater and a copier, a leader and a follower. Buermann was determined to sell his products to horsemen everywhere, and he succeeded. Whatever type of spur was in demand, Buermann attempted to meet that demand. He manufactured California, Mexican, and Texas spurs, military and police spurs, English and jockey spurs, cheap spurs and expensive, hand-forged, silver-inlaid spurs.

The Buermann Company was advertised as being founded in 1842, the year Buermann himself was born, on November 4, in Sattenhausen in the District of Gottingen, Kingdom of Hannover, Germany. After his early schooling he spent four years in apprenticeship to a locksmith in Hamburg, where he also enrolled in a business course. Not content with limited knowledge, he continued his studies until he was recognized as a "practical mechanic" in several trades. After traveling his native land, visiting the larger cities and industrial areas, he decided that there was still more of the world to see before he settled down, so he booked passage in 1863 on a small ship sailing from Bremerhaven to New York. He arrived on August 18 and a few days later in Newark, New Jersey, became an employee in the Market Street factory of Alexander Barclay, manufacturer of saddlery hardware since 1842.[2]

Buermann was quickly caught up in the fervor of the Civil War being waged in his new country. On September 13, 1864, he enlisted as a private in the Ninth Regiment of the New Jersey Volunteers, commanded by Gen. John M. Schofield. After the war, August was honorably discharged and returned to Newark, where he was again associated with Alexander Barclay. But he had plans of his own, and in 1866 he purchased the Barclay business. On April 3, 1868, he married Margaretha Koenig, also a native of Germany.[3]

By 1870, Buermann and a partner in the saddlery hardware business, August Hartmann, were operating as Buermann & Hartmann at 83-85 Hamilton Street.

Hartmann may have been involved in the acquisition of the Barclay Company, but by 1880 Buermann was the full owner of the business, which was then located at 37-39 New Jersey Railroad Avenue, and Hartmann had become a locksmith. There were only sixty-eight saddlery hardware manufacturers in the entire United States in 1888, and the Buermann Company was one of twenty-five located in Newark. August Buermann was an enterprising young man, creative and ambitious, and his business flourished from the beginning.[4]

By 1896 the Buermann Company had one hundred employees.[5] It eventually outgrew its original facilities, and by 1906 it had built a new four-story plant at 220-224 Jelliff Avenue adjoining the westbound branch of the Pennsylvania Railroad, thus making shipping facilities more accessible.

Buermann was frugal yet innovative. He kept his factory up to date with the latest equipment and was recognized as one of the pioneers in the manufacture of bits and spurs in the United States. His business prospered, and he eventually had funds to invest in real estate, organizing an investment company and buying property in the most desirable residential areas of Newark. One of the pioneer developers of the Clinton Hill section of the city, he paid for cutting the streets through the area and improving them. As one of the founders of the Fourteenth Ward Building and Loan Company, he helped finance many homes. He was also an organizer and director of the Clinton Trust Company. His civic interests were widespread. He was a director of a home for the aged, a long-time trustee of the First German Baptist Church, and a member of the Board of Trade and the Newark Chamber of Commerce.[6]

Buermann's son August, Jr., involved in the manufacturing company from 1896 at the age of nineteen, succeeded August as president shortly after graduating from New Jersey Business College. Eventually August, Jr., also became vice-president and then president of the Buermann Investment Company. He retired from the manufacturing company in 1926 when it was sold to North & Judd.[7]

Like North & Judd—his competitor, predecessor, and, later, acquirer—Buermann sold strictly to jobbers and wholesalers,[8] but he emphasized his spur, bit, and stirrup lines much more than North & Judd did, for they carried a wider range of hardware.

Buermann was a person of inventive genius who patented his designs and modifications. On August 12, 1879, he registered his trademark, the Star Brand, which was to be stamped on spurs and printed on letterheads, labels, and such. In his declaration he stated, "This trademark I have used in my business for the twenty months last past." The "star" was registered a second time as trademark no. 9356 on May 16, 1882, and again on September 24, 1912.

On February 6, 1877, he received patent no. 186,985 for a flange on the heel band to prevent the chain brackets that swung from the button studs on some of his spurs from rotating around the buttons and twisting the instep chains. On March 18, 1879, he patented design no. 11,080, the Excelsior, a style that was used for many years. It was advertised in the Sears, Roebuck and Company catalog of 1897 and was still in Buermann's catalog in the 1920s. Also patented on March 30, 1880, and again on May 1, 1883, was the Buermann Eureka Plain, with a large star on the outside of the heel band. In 1882 this spur was pictured on Buermann's second application for the Star Brand trademark. He continued his policy of patenting various spur styles

Star overstamped with B on A; HAND FORGED STEEL and PAT'D stamped in heel band of each spur. Shown as No. 2024 in Buermann Catalog no. 35 (1922). Half-mounted with silver and copper; heel bands scalloped on top; swinging heart buttons. *Huff Collection; photo by Bob L. Trantham.*

Star overstamped with B on A under buttons and PAT'D inside heel bands. Hercules Bronze with Nickel Silver ornaments. Spur No. 1382½ (patented) "Lone Star" in Buermann Catalog no. 35. *Mitchell Collection.*

throughout the existence of the company. When the firm was sold in 1926, the Star Brand trademark was assigned to North & Judd, and it finally went to Gulf & Western Precision Engineering of New York when that corporation acquired North & Judd in 1967.[9]

Buermann also developed two metals for the exclusive use of his company: Hercules Bronze and Star Steel Silver. Whereas his first spurs, European and military types, were undoubtedly made from the traditional solid brass, iron, or malleable iron, his later work featured these two nonrusting alloys, compounded of several metals for strength. Spurs made of these materials were cast and of the same composition throughout. The 1922 catalog stated that all Buermann spurs made with Star Steel Silver had that name stamped on them.[10]

The Buermann company had its own foundry, and most Star Brand spurs were cast, but it also had a hand-forged line. Catalogs advertised that the Star Brand on Buermann spurs and bits corresponded to the Sterling mark on silver. The trademark on Buermann's catalog is a star with an A on one side and a B on the other and "Trade Mark" printed under it. A B over-stamped on an A inside a star marked many Buermann spurs on the outside of the heel band near the button. Some Buermann spurs also have the word PATENTED stamped inside the heel band. Others are stamped FORGED STEEL. In some styles, PAT'D is stamped back under the button.[11]

Collectors will also find spurs that are stamped with an arm and hammer on the heel band under the button. Spurs with this mark may have been Buermann's hand-forged products. The arm and hammer in a black diamond is pictured in Buermann's *Catalog no. 35* (1922) as a Buermann trademark registered with the U.S. Patent Office, but a similar trademark on a white diamond was used by J. R. McChesney. A reproduction of McChesney's trademark appears beside a picture of a McChesney gal-leg spur in the 1913 Charles P. Shipley Saddlery & Mercantile Company.[12] None of the McChesney family recalls that McChesney used this stamp on any of his spurs, but spurs carrying it are recognized as McChesney styles, and the same styles are also seen in the Buermann catalog.

Beside the arm and hammer Buermann trademark in *Catalog no. 35* is printed the following:

The Most Complete Line of
Hand Forged Steel
Fine Silver Inlaid Bits and Spurs

> All our bits and spurs are inlaid with Finest Coil silver. This is done only
> by hand, by the most experienced and expert workmen. This silver is NOT
> SOLDERED ON, but is hand hammered in the forgings before the finished
> process, which makes it extremely secure and serviceable. Many years of
> experience doing this class of work has made the "Star Brand" Hand Made
> Silver Inlaid Bits and Spurs the best that money can buy.

The craftmanship of Buermann products won awards for excellence from the Centennial Commission of Philadelphia in 1876. This was a competition not of one manufacturer against another, but against a standard, with recognition by a panel of judges for high-quality products in various categories. Star Brand products also received awards at the World Industrial and Cotton Centennial Exposition in New Orleans in 1884–85, at the Pan American Exposition in Buffalo in 1902, and at the 1904 Saint Louis World's Fair.[13]

Despite Buermann's innovativeness, the company was not hesitant to absorb new ideas from other sources. When western spur makers like McChesney of Texas, Oscar Crockett of Kansas and Colorado, P. M. Kelly of Texas, and others fired up their forges in the early 1900s and developed their own styles for the cowboys' delight, these Texas-style spur makers cut into the Buermann Company's business. The company was far removed from its western customers' whims and changes of styles, so it soon began to follow the lead of these craftsmen, including their most popular

Star overstamped with B on A under swinging buttons. Same configuration as No. 1115 in Buermann Catalog no. 35. Chap guards and 1⅛-inch heel band. Hand-forged and silver-mounted. Eighteen-point rowels. *Huber Collection; photo by Dwight Huber.*

designs among the products listed in its catalog. Some said that Buermann not only copied competitors' spurs but even lifted the pictures of particular spurs directly from competitors' catalogs to use in his own.[14]

Whereas Kelly, McChesney, and their contemporaries made cowboy spurs, and West Coast craftsmen made the inlaid buckaroo spurs, the Buermann Company tried to keep up with all of them. It made Texas, California, English, and military spurs. Among its Dom Pedro line, one spur was particularly popular with cowboys. It was patterned after the style known in the United States as the Chihuahua spur and cast in one piece, with heavy, twisted-looking heel bands ending in big open rings from which the flower-shaped buttons swung.[15]

Buermann's Catalog no. 35 pictured 443 spur designs and almost as many bits. In 1926, when the North & Judd Company bought out Buermann, it discontinued many spurs and bits. P. M. Kelly's perception was that the hand-forged line was dropped and only the patented spurs were continued.

If August Buermann had never made another style, the O.K. spur would have perpetuated his name in western history. This spur is associated with the Buermann name even though others also made O.K. spurs, and its original designer was probably Texas gunsmith J. C. Petmecky.[16] Their popularity is shown by the words of the cowboy song, "Little Joe, the Wrangler":

> His saddle 'twas a southern kack built many years ago.
> An O.K. spur on one foot idly hung,
> While his "hot roll" in a cotton sack was loosely tied behind,
> And a canteen from the saddle horn he'd slung.[17]

It has been said that O.K. spurs date back to Civil War times, but none was patented until long after that. A spur of that configuration was patented by Buermann on July 6, 1886. On March 20, 1888, Buermann was also awarded a patent on design no. 18187, an O.K. spur with a straight, short, wide shank and four buttons. An O.K. spur patented in 1908 by Star Steel Spur Company of Wastego, Illinois, had a shank that was a little different from the other designs.[18] On a page of O.K. spurs from a Buermann catalog reproduced in a catalog published by Wyeth Hardware and Manufacturing Company of Saint Joseph, Missouri, these spurs ranged from $6.50 to $8.00 a dozen for blued styles and $10.00 a dozen for nickel-plated ones, or from 55 cents to 85 cents a pair, which would fit any cowboy's pay of a dollar a day and grub.

Buermann made several styles of O.K. spurs. The classic O.K. had a short, curved, raised shank, but there were also straight shanks. Both styles were made in two-button and four-button models. The heel band was fairly wide at the shank and tapered down to smooth, curved ends. The O.K. is stamped into the heel band near the shank, and on this classic style, BUERMANN'S is stamped in a crescent over the O.K.[19] This style of spurs was still advertised in Buermann's catalog of 1922, but by then the O.K. had lost its popularity with those who could afford Buermann's hand-forged spurs or the custom-made spurs offered by the cowboy spur makers of the early twentieth century.

Margaretha Buermann died on March 11, 1911, in Newark. August lived to the age of eighty-six and died on November 2, 1928, at his home in East Orange. August had lived to see the death of his son George in 1922 and the sale of the Star Brand company he had built and made internationally famous.

Though the August Buermann Manufacturing Company ceased to exist in 1926, the Star Brand continued to mark the products developed and made famous by the young German immigrant who came to the United States in search of opportunity. Even though his life and business were in the East, his products influenced the West, and his spurs and bits can now be found in collections throughout the country, so August Buermann's dream lives on.

Chapter 4

The Anchor Brand of North & Judd

The Anchor brand stamped on spurs and bits, as well as many other hardware items, has denoted products made by North & Judd Manufacturing Company of Connecticut since 1878, but the company has a much longer history. According to its tradition, the business was founded in 1812, but its beginning was actually before 1800, when James North operated a well-known blacksmith shop on Main Street in New Britain.[1] The community was a center of activity even at that time, having cobblers, sawmills, grist mills that ground corn to be shipped to the West Indies, tinware shops, and numerous blacksmith shops in which craftsmen made nails, axes, hoes, chains, and such.

New Britain was making its mark as a business center, which surprised outsiders, for the town was not near water for power or transportation, and it had no forests, mines, vineyards, or agriculture, all thought necessary for prosperity. When asked what the advantages of New Britain were, an inhabitant is said to have answered, "The grace of God and men like Major North!"

James North became interested in the brass business in 1800, and with his son James and a man named Shipman he began making brass sleigh bells in his shop at the corner of South Main and Park streets. Another son, Seth, soon joined them in the brass business, and before long the shops of North & Shipman were recognized as the leading manufacturers of sleigh bells in the country.

In 1808, Hezekiah C. Whipple of Providence, Rhode Island, came to New Britain to work for a jewelry company, and in 1810 or 1811 Whipple bought his own shop and began making silver-plated harness buckles, cloak clasps, and plated wire for hooks and eyes and rings for clothing. At that time shaping the wire was all handwork. Along with his brother Alvin, Seth North became a partner with Whipple, and the Norths introduced the use of horse power to operate machines. Following the War of 1812, Alvin North bought out his partners. By 1822 he had a new partner, Horace Butler. Their business expanded to include the manufacture of such articles as brass curb chains and harness rings. About 1830 a machine for the shaping of wire articles was made in Hartford, and shortly after that North had one in New Britain. Butler bought North's interest in 1832 and continued in business for a number of years.

After North sold out to Butler, he went into business on his own, making small articles of cast brass and saddlery hardware. In the early 1840s Alvin's son Oliver B. joined him, and the company became known as A. North & Sons, expand-

The North & Judd Manufacturing Company of New Britain, Connecticut, 1892. *Photo from* In and About New Britain, *courtesy Connecticut Historical Society.*

ing from the manufacture of cast brass articles and harness buckles of ironwire to saddlery hardware made of malleable iron. In 1849 Oliver sold his interest to his brother Hubert F. North, whose partnership with his father continued until May 17, 1855. At that time Lorin F. Judd and James A. Pickett bought Alvin North's interest and with Hubert North formed H. F. North & Company. At that time, the firm employed thirty men.

During the Civil War the company did a large business in furnishing the U.S. Army with a ton of goods daily, week after week, including trimming for two million knapsacks. It is reported that the company sold well over $250,000 worth of goods to the government. This prosperity led to incorporation as North & Judd Manufacturing Company, with a capital of $60,000, on September 24, 1863. Hubert North was quite feeble, and his activity in the company was limited to serving as a member of the board of directors. Judd was president and Pickett secretary-treasurer.

North & Judd at that time was housed in a wooden building on the corner of East Main and Stanley streets. On December 16, 1864, a fire started in the japanning rooms, in the benzine used in that coating process, and burned a portion of the factory. It was soon rebuilt and enlarged in what was reported at the time to be "a fireproof and very substantial manner." In 1866 a new building was added.

In 1888 the supposedly fireproof factory burned to the ground, and this time it was replaced by a brick structure. In 1900 the company had 500 employees; by 1925 more than 1,200 were employed; and by 1945 the North & Judd plant covered 587,000 square feet on 13½ acres and had several thousand employees.

Anchor stamped by button; five nickel spots along outside heel bands. Available in iron, solid Gun Metal, or blued. Shown as Spur No. 1911 in Catalog no. 83 (1914) with 1¾-inch cast rowels. Spur design patented June 20, 1911, by James W. Keyston, Jr., of San Francisco, assignor to North & Judd. The same spur was made with three nickel spots. *Mitchell Collection.*

North & Judd's famous Anchor Brand trademark for saddlery hardware was registered with the U.S. Patent Office on April 15, 1879, as trademark no. 7,201. The statement as filed on March 14, 1879, reads in part: "This trademark has been used by said company for about six months past. The class of merchandise to which it is appropriated is known as 'saddlery hardware,' and the particular descriptions of goods upon which it is intended to use said trademark are buckles, rings, bits, terrets, cheek-hooks, bolt-hooks, and other hardware for harness-makers' and saddlers' use generally; and it has been printed in faint colors cornerwise over the body of various labels, which labels have been pasted on said articles or boxes."

Just when North & Judd began making bits and spurs has been forgotten, but according to Shirley Muter, who is with the firm, it appears to have been during the 1830s, for old literature states that at that time they "tried to satisfy the needs of the rider."[2] Of the dozen or so spurs that were patented between 1790 and 1873, none were by North & Judd or any of the men forming partnerships in the parent companies. In the patent records from 1877 through 1924, North & Judd, though not the original patentee, appears often as assignee for designs patented by other individuals, such as Fredrick C. Monier of New Britain and J. W. Keyston, Jr., of San Francisco, a noted maker of buckaroo spurs. Keyston's well-known Five Spot spur was assigned to North & Judd on June 20, 1911.

During the Spanish American War, North & Judd supplied the government's needs on a large scale, and the army also purchased great quantities of Anchor Brand products throughout World War I. Following the war, North & Judd received an award from the secretary of war for "distinguished service, loyalty, energy, and efficiency in performance, which aided materially in obtaining victory for the army of the United States of America."[3]

After the war the firm continued to flourish, and in 1919 it began buying other businesses of like type, beginning with W. & E. T. Fitch Company of New

Haven. In 1925 it purchased the Traut & Hine Manufacturing Company of New Britain, and the following year it added the August Buermann Company. By 1929 North & Judd had branch offices in New York, Chicago, Saint Louis, San Francisco, Detroit, and Toronto. [4]

The O. B. North Company of New Haven, after being a separate entity since 1849, was bought from Oliver North's heirs and returned to the fold in 1930, the same year that North & Judd acquired the United States Hame Company of Buffalo, New York. In 1933, North & Judd purchased the Spot Division from the Beardsley & Wolcott Company of Waterbury, Connecticut. The list of acquisitions goes on and on. [5] The corporation was a conglomerate of its day, consolidating many lines of hardware under its famous Anchor Brand, and because of its far-sighted officers and the diversification of its products, it remains in business and continues to grow. The firm has always been a wholesaler, selling only to the original equipment manufacturers or distributors and never retail. In 1950 it became a subsidiary of the giant Gulf & Western Precision Engineering Company of New York. [6]

In more recent times the North & Judd plant was moved to Middletown, Connecticut, when a new highway system was to be built through New Britain and over the site of the old factory. In Middletown, North & Judd is housed under one roof with a sister company, Wilcox-Crittendon, manufacturers of marine hardware since 1847. [7]

In speaking of North & Judd's spur-making process, Shirley Muter states:

> Even going back to the 1830s, almost everything was cast, since molding is a very old process. When spurs became a major line, even though they were cast, 70 percent of the line had hand engraving after the casting process in the foundry, and we even did silver inlay and custom work. At one time we had some hand-forged spurs as well as cast ones. We had our own brass foundry and iron foundry in New Britain. When we moved to Middletown, we moved the brass foundry into an old Wilcox building, but we now have the iron castings made by a sister company. [8]

North & Judd still has many of the patterns used in casting.

The various styles of North & Judd spurs were available in brass or bronze alloys or in malleable iron. The malleable iron spurs were either blued, electro-brass plated, XC plated, or nickeled. Some spurs were cast in solid brass, and others were solid Gun Metal with white nickel ornamentation. White nickel was a hard, malleable, ductile metal that could be molded or hammered into thin layers; the Solid White Nickel alloy was the Anchor brand's version of Buermann's Star Steel Silver. Some styles of spurs were engraved, and others were chased. Some spurs were simply burnished or polished to make them shiny. [9]

In 1926 North & Judd acquired the Buermann Company, long a major competitor of the Anchor Brand's line of spurs, bits, and stirrups. A comparison of the catalogs of the two firms reveals many duplications. Possibly Buermann did contract work for the larger concern. When North & Judd purchased the New Jersey company, many of the top-selling Buermann styles were continued and their stock numbers appeared in the North & Judd catalogs with the prefix *B*. [10]

The famous Buermann trademark, the star, was transferred to the new

Stamped PAT'D inside heel bands and with a plain star under the outside buttons, indicating a Buermann spur now made by North & Judd. Made of Hercules Bronze with Nickel Silver horse head ornaments. Prior to North & Judd's acquisition of the Buermann Company in 1926, this style was made of Gun Metal. *Huff Collection; photo by Bob L. Trantham.*

owners and continued to appear on the spurs and bits that it had long marked.[11] Shirley Muter notes:

> When we acquired the Buermann Company, we continued to use their patterns. Buermann's mark, the B stamped over the A in the center of the star, was made into those patterns. Details can be filed off of a pattern, but they cannot be added, so the A and B were filed off, and we continued using the old patterns with a plain star. Our spurs and bits were primarily marked either with the star, the anchor, or STAR STEEL SILVER. Many of our bits were made of solid white nickel, which is akin to Star Steel Silver, which we acquired with the purchase of the Buermann company as we did Hercules Bronze.

North & Judd did not immediately drop the Buermann name on acquisition of the company. Their catalog no. 36 (no date) is called *Supplementary Catalog—Buermann Line.* Catalog no. 37 has on the cover "High Grade Bits, Spurs & Miscellaneous Hardware. Star Brand," with A ☆ B. Catalog no. 38 is titled *High Grade Bits, Spurs & Stirrups & Miscellaneous Hardware—The Buermann Line with Additions.* Catalog no. 39 is *Bits, Spurs, Stirrups—English & Western,* and Buermann's name no longer appears. It does say "Made in New England by North & Judd Manufacturing Company—Anchor Brand and Star Brand Products." In catalog no. 93 the line is advertised as Star Steel Silver Riding Hardware.[12] Evidently there was a gradual phasing out of the Buermann name. New pieces were added in the catalogs, but some old styles from the Buermann catalogs were continued. Besides the marks mentioned, some pieces were stamped TESTED, FORGED STEEL, MADE IN NEW ENGLAND, PAT'D, PATENTED, or STAR ☆ BRAND.

Stamped with Anchor brand. Made of Solid Gun Metal. Turned-up heel band; two stationary buttons; 1¼-inch steel twenty-point rowels. Note Anchor brand on heel band. *Huff Collection; photo by Bob L. Trantham.*

Spurs, which had long been a major item of manufacture, were phased out beginning about 1963, but even before then, North & Judd's spur line had been reduced drastically. The 1953 catalog, no. 93, pictured only eleven spurs, nine made of Star Steel Silver and two of Hercules Bronze with Nickel Silver ornamentation. Four were English-style spurs. Several of the spurs were marked STAR ☆ BRAND inside the heel band, and two still carried the star by the button and PAT'D in the heel band. STAR ☆ BRAND was also printed under some styles of bits. [13]

Two styles of bits and spurs, the buffalo head and the horse head, still appeared in the catalogs after 1963 as special-order items. Both styles were developed by Buermann and were marketed by North & Judd individually or together as the Royal Roundup Set. North & Judd finally discontinued even these styles in 1982. Similar spurs, but made of Gun Metal with white nickel ornamentation, had been sold by North & Judd as the Buffalo Bill Ranchman's Set. In catalog no. 83 a letter appeared, written in 1912 to North & Judd from William "Buffalo Bill" Cody, stating, "The last bit you sent me is pronounced by my cowboys and myself as the most practicable and humane bit we have ever seen. I am using it on my favorite horse. We call it the 'Perfect Bit.'" Cody's endorsement of Anchor Brand bits was given a full-page spread. [14]

North & Judd made several unique bits as well, including the Colt .45, which had cheek pieces made in the shape of full-sized Colts. This design was patented by Buffalo Bill Cody in 1916, and North & Judd became the assignee. Few of these were made, but the style was a catalog special-order item. A bit of this design with Cody's signature on the cheek piece is on exhibit at the Buffalo Bill Museum in Cody, Wyoming. The same style bit, stamped several times with the Buermann star with the AB in the center, is in the collection of Ralph Emerson, Jr., and the bit can also be found marked STAR STEEL SILVER above the trigger and with an anchor and a coil of rope in a rosette on the lip bar.

Today according to Shirley Muter, "We're into the saddlery or equestrian-type business, but make no horse jewelry other than a few working-type bits." In 1984, North & Judd's line consisted of buckles; rings; hardware for nylon horse halters and rope halters for cows; chains of stainless steel, brass, iron, and steel; industrial hardware; turnbuckles and forgings; hand trucks; fasteners and hardware for luggage; sporting goods; and life preservers. Advertising before World War II stated, "Nine times out of ten, if it's a small hardware part, North & Judd makes it." [15] That is even more true today.

When the firm moved from its long-time home in New Britain to Middletown, many of its old records were destroyed or lost. All that are left, including old patterns for spurs, bits, and other items, are locked away in the archives. Because of the loss of much material, facts and dates concerning early-day spur making often are only tradition and have become scantier as memories fade and younger generations take up the reins. Whereas family-oriented businesses often retain their histories, large corporations need someone like Shirley Muter to preserve an active interest in days gone by.

Chapter 5

John Robert McChesney, Granddaddy of the Texas-Style Spur

If any man deserves to be called the granddaddy of the style known as the Texas spur, it would have to be John Robert McChesney, who was the first to market handmade Texas spurs. He hammered his first spurs out of hot steel in Indian Territory in 1887.[1] Hoping his business would expand enough that he would need the shipping facilities of a railroad town, he moved in 1890 to Gainesville, Texas, and then in 1910 to Pauls Valley, Oklahoma, where the McChesney Bit & Spur Company operated as a respected leader in the field.

McChesney was born on September 29, 1866, in South Bend, Indiana, lived there until he was eighteen years old, then traveled with his parents by wagon train to Rogers, Arkansas.[2] While in Rogers, he met and married Tabitha Thomas. In 1887 they moved to the settlement of Broken Arrow, south of the young Indian Territory town of Tulsa.

Broken Arrow was a gathering place for ranchers. Their buggies and wagons were always in need of repairs, and horses had to be shod regularly, so a good smithy was never idle. When McChesney heard of a blacksmith shop in Tulsa that could be bought for five dollars, he walked there to buy it. After he purchased it, he was offered the deed to five city blocks in Tulsa if he would stay there and keep the business in operation, but he declined. Instead, he found a man with a wagon and an ox team who agreed to haul the dismantled shop and equipment to Broken Arrow for fifty cents.

McChesney was a jack-of-all-trades where ironwork was concerned, and his business flourished almost before he could get set up. He set wagon wheels, repaired guns, made branding irons, and shod horses, often in exchange for goods rather than cash. The story was passed down in the family that he often traded guns and horses with desperadoes who frequented the Indian Territory and that the outlaw Belle Starr was a welcome guest in the McChesneys' one-room log house, as she was in many homes in the area.[3]

Broken Arrow was a typical frontier settlement with all the aspects of a wild cow town. The neighboring ranchers and their cowhands were often in town. One cowman made a nuisance of himself trying to persuade the blacksmith to make him a pair of spurs. Business was good, and McChesney kept putting him off, even though the man said he'd pay any price to get the spurs. On his next visit, he punctuated his plea by shooting through the roof of the blacksmith shop.

A few days later McChesney got his work caught up and decided to make the spurs for his wild friend. He took two teeth from an old harrow, split each tooth partway, and hammered and shaped the split sections to fit a boot heel. Then he cut a piece off each shank, hammered it out, and filed rowel spokes into it. When the rancher came to town the next trip, he was surprised to find his spurs ready, and did not bat an eye at paying five dollars for them. He was so pleased, in fact, that he offered to pay five dollars for a matching bit. So another harrow tooth was split on each end and worked into a one-piece bit. The spurs had paid for the shop, and the bit had made the blacksmith five dollars to boot.

One morning soon afterwards McChesney heard a big ruckus outside as a group of cowboys rode up to his shop firing their pistols and hurrahing. He stepped outside and asked the meaning of the commotion. The cowboys replied, "We want to order some spurs, and ol' Bill said you wouldn't make any unless we shot off our pistols and raised Cain!"

It did not take that kind of persuasion to get McChesney to agree to take their orders, for he had now learned that spur making could be lucrative. He invited the boys to step down from their horses and come inside, where he took fifty orders for spurs and bits, cash with the orders. Once again McChesney walked to Tulsa, where he bought three hundred pounds of harrow teeth, freighting them back to Broken Arrow. After he shipped those spurs and bits, he was flooded with new orders.[4] It is said that while in Indian Territory McChesney originated the goose-neck spur. This style was copied, but not as extensively as the gal-leg, which some people say McChesney also originated.[5] Cowboys seemed to prefer gals' legs to the necks of geese.

In the late 1880s a severe drought had hurt many Texas cattlemen who ran herds on the grasslands of Indian Territory, and barbed wire had ended the great trail drives. These developments probably influenced McChesney's decision to move his business in 1890 to the flourishing community of Gainesville, Texas. With the coming of the railroads, Gainesville had become a lively trade center and one of the most important cattle shipping points of North Texas. By 1890 the town had telephones and telegraph, electric lights, cement sidewalks, graveled streets, and incandescent street lamps, and the railroads gave local businesses access to all corners of the country.[6] Certain of the merchants there enjoyed a large retail and wholesale liquor business, shipping wagon load after wagon load of spirits north across the Red River to Indian Territory, Kansas, and Missouri.[7]

McChesney's first shop, a small rectangular building, was located on Rice Avenue south of the downtown area and near the race track at the fair grounds, and the McChesney family lived nearby. McChesney made bits and spurs, but he was primarily concerned with general blacksmith work, and he shod the race horses and the trotters and pacers from the track. He also did repair work and specialized in bicycles.[8] In 1901, when the town's streetcar line was discontinued, McChesney bought one of the line's three cars and added it to his facilities on Rice Avenue.[9] There were soon five or six men in the shop. When the Santa Fe Railroad purchased the site

The first page of the J. R. McChesney *Spur and Bit Catalog* for 1906 pictured the company's founder. *Courtesy National Cowboy Hall of Fame.*

of the fair grounds to mine gravel for use on road beds, the race track was moved to the north side of town.

That triggered McChesney's move to a new location in the northeast part of Gainesville, where he built on the corner of Taylor and Olive streets. Double doors in the side of the building opened to the north onto Olive. In 1896 a Y-shaped float bridge had been built across Pecan Creek to the east of the Gainesville business section. Kirby McPherson, whose brother Matt worked part-time for McChesney, recalled: "The McChesney shop was at the very end of North Taylor Street near one fork of the Y Bridge. It was a long, one-story building with a wooden floor. My aunt and uncle lived near there, and I'd often stop by the shop, and Mr. McChesney would pay me a dime to sweep out."[10]

It was at this location that the general blacksmithing was forgotten, and J. R. McChesney Spurs and Bits truly came into being, and it was from there that the company issued its first catalog in 1906.[11] McChesney was a good friend of H. J. Justin, the noted boot maker in Nocona, Texas. Enid Justin, his daughter and the president of Nocona Boot Company, recalled, "My father also cataloged Mr. McChesney's bits and spurs in his little boot catalog while the McChesney Company was still in Gainesville." The two families were friends, and one of the older McChesney sons, John, made trips to Nocona to visit Enid.[12]

James Madison (Matt) McPherson worked in the Gainesville foundry and worked for McChesney after hours and on weekends making molds for bits and spurs. His younger brother Kirby recalled that the molds were good only for limited use and then had to be reworked. "Matt used black sand in a mold, and the red-hot iron was poured into that," Kirby remembered. "Then the rough spur was dressed down, polished, and decorated. Matt was a horseshoer, a blacksmith, and a machinist. He had learned the trade in Boots Blacksmith Shop on Main and Rusk streets across from the Bischoff Carriage Works. Three or four men worked part-time for McChesney, including the brother of the owner of the iron foundry."[13] Milt Dickerman sweated on silver, copper, or brass decorations, and the engraving was done by Louie Brontz, a marble cutter who did the fancy work on tombstones for a living and engraved for McChesney after hours. Bob Carnell, a saddle maker, did the bridle work for the McChesney bits. "I recall McChesney as being tall and slender," McPherson said, "and I never saw him when he didn't have on bib overalls."

There were several retail outlets in Gainesville for McChesney products: Tramblade's Second-hand Store, A. H. Ross and Son Hardware Store, and Cheaney's Livery Stable. Stephens, Kennerly & Spraguns, a firm that handled lumber, hardware, and windmills, had a display of the McChesney goods in a glass showcase.[14] While Gainesville prospered, so did McChesney, but the town's decline began in 1903 when the local option provision caused the exodus of liquor dealers. By 1910 only a few alcoholic beverage dealers remained in Gainesville after more than forty saloons and most of the wholesale houses had moved to Fort Worth and Dallas. The town's population dropped drastically,[15] and the decline of commerce most likely forced McChesney to search for a better location for his spur business.

As Gainesville withered, Pauls Valley, to the north in the new state of Oklahoma, geared up for a boom. The Pauls Valley Chamber of Commerce induced McChesney to move there. McChesney bought a city block for $4,500 right across from the railroad depot. He planned to establish a foundry and also operate his bit and spur business. Some of his workers moved to Oklahoma with him, including his brother-in-law, Charlie Roberts, who was married to McChesney's sister Nat and had accompanied him from Arkansas.[16] By 1910 Pauls Valley had its first brick paving, and McChesney built a two-story concrete shop on the corner of South Earl and East Charles streets.

P. M. Kelly, a young man with a thriving blacksmith business in Hansford, Texas, had met McChesney in Fort Worth in 1907 in the Tandy Leather Company office. McChesney had made some punch presses for leather bridle blinds for work

John Robert
McChesney

———

45

Inside the McChesney shop in Paul's Valley. *Courtesy National Cowboy Hall of Fame.*

horses and was there to sell them to Tandy. When Kelly later visited the McChesney shop in Gainesville, the owner offered him a job, but Kelly had a good business going and declined at that time. Later, in 1910, Kelly decided to move to Dalhart and expand his bit and spur business, but only after learning what he could from McChesney.

Kelly began working for McChesney as head forger the day after the shop opened in Pauls Valley. He replaced Albert Dickerman, who had remained in Gainesville. "I was one of Mac's highest paid employees," Kelly recalled, "because he found I could do more than what he hired me for, and he wanted machine work done. He had lathes, shapers, and drill presses, and I was kept busy making dies and tools." Kelly had worked on steam and gasoline engines and windmills in Texas, and he and another employee, Clyde Parker, were soon busy not just in the shop but also after hours on hay balers and other equipment. McChesney insisted that they keep for themselves all the money earned after hours. Kelly and McChesney worked well together, but in 1911, after nine months, Kelly felt that he was ready to go back into business for himself. McChesney hated to lose him, but he sold him an unfinished punch press casting to help him get started.

Once Kelly got tooled up for production in Dalhart, several of McChesney's men left to work for him, including Tom Johnson, Jr., Clyde Parker, and J. R. Barker. Charlie Roberts became McChesney's head forger, and Bill McChesney was his father's mainstay and engraver.[17] All of McChesney's sons—J. D. Bill, Henry, Amos (who was known as Monk), Tom, Bob, and Frank—worked in the shop at one time or another. The four girls, Maud, Fay, May, and Rosetta, ran the office at various times.

Full-mounted McChesney gal-leg spurs. The outside heel band is decorated with a bouquet of silver prairie tulips and leaves. The inside heel band has a silver-plate overlay with copper leaves inlaid. The leg on the inside of the shank is flat; outside is rounded. Turned-up buttons. Unmarked. *Huff Collection.*

The bit and spur operation was on the first floor of the building behind the office, and for awhile the McChesney family lived upstairs over the back. Later, McChesney built several houses behind his factory, and some of the family lived in them. Mac loved to cook, and his home was often full of young people and friends.[18]

During this period, he employed as many as fifty people and catalogued 120 patterns of spurs and 64 bridle bits, which were sold through large and small jobbers and shipped to all parts of the world. He made spurs for many noted people, including Will Rogers, the famous bronc rider "Booger Red," Col. Jim Eskew, and Floyd and Florence Randolph of rodeo fame. "My father was well-known for his gal-leg spurs with copper socks, silver garters and silver slippers," Robert McChesney, John's sixth son, recalled.[19]

In 1917 Charlie Roberts's son-in-law, Joe Willard, went to work roughing out spurs in the factory. His job was to put almost molten steel in a die and drop the top die to shape a spur. Then he and W. D. Barnett would grind the pieces to smooth them. Next, each spur would go to the polisher and, last, to the engraver. It was an assembly-line operation. There was also a bit-maker. During this period the shop employed about eight men and a secretary, who was usually one of the McChesney girls. Willard earned fifteen cents an hour for a ten-hour day, six days a week. Roberts got top pay of five dollars to six dollars a day.[20]

"John McChesney had great ideas," Willard said, "but by this time, he'd develop something, but he wouldn't follow through on it. He'd go to something else. At one time, he built an excursion boat and put it on the Washita River. The river had to be up to float it, and then he couldn't get it under thr bridge. He soon forgot that and decided to put in a hotel upstairs over the factory. That was short-lived, too. . . . McChesney had a successful business in the bit and spur venture, but at this point, he

John Robert
McChesney

_____

47

didn't follow up on his orders, and his business soon began to drop off." As business slacked, the men worked only five days, then four, then three. Finally the McChesney boys left for the oil fields to make their living.[21]

"By the time I worked for McChesney," Willard pointed out, "many of the spur makers were machining up for faster production. McChesney's products continued to be hand-forged and hand-worked. The gal-leg spurs sold for $5.00, but you could buy a facsimile for $2.25. Of course, they weren't the McChesney quality either, but that still cut into his business."

During World War I, McChesney landed a government contract to make bits and spurs for the army. This required a piece of equipment that cost a sizable sum for those days. The machinery was delivered only a short time before the war ended, however, leaving McChesney with a cancelled contract and a large debt. Perhaps this money pressure caused him to neglect his spur business and encouraged him to seek to earn money with the hotel and excursion boat. Perhaps it also contributed to his death from a heart attack at the age of sixty-two on January 8, 1928.[22]

One of McChesney's successful sidelines to his spurs and bits had been an auto salvage and repair business he operated in his shop, reportedly one of the largest in that section of the state. The family tried to continue both spur making and auto salvage, but business was not good. On November 4, 1929, the factory building and property were acquired by the First National Bank and Trust Company of Oklahoma City.[23] For more than half a century, the building remained empty, and until about 1980 the sign MCCHESNEY'S SPURS & BITS, painted across the top of the building with linseed oil and lamp black, could still be seen.

"Shortly after John McChesney's death," Enid Justin said, "Mrs. McChesney contacted me about buying the business. I owned the Nocona Boot Company of Nocona, Texas, and we bought the McChesney name, equipment, and stock. Five men and their families came from Pauls Valley with the company. They were W. D. "Slim" Barnett, Jim Welch, W. T. Ray, a Mr. Cash, and a Mr. Ballinger. Slim Barnett had worked for McChesney for a number of years as his head engraver." Nocona Boot Company Catalog No. 8 included McChesney products: thirteen styles of spurs and five designs of bits. It was only during the time McChesney products were made in Nocona that spurs were plated. They were also stamped MCCHESNEY in small letters under the button. "By 1933 four of the five men who had moved from Pauls Valley had either died or left the company," Enid Justin recalled. "With them went their knowledge of spur making, so we were forced to close the bit and spur business. Slim Barnett stayed on with us in the boot factory as a machinist." Most of the McChesney equipment and dies were finally acquired by Adolph Bayers of Truscott, Texas, a craftsman of whose workmanship John McChesney would have approved. Many of those dies are now in the Panhandle-Plains Historical Museum, Canyon, Texas. The McChesney business papers, which were in the possession of son T. C., were lost when his house burned.[24]

McChesney spurs are easily recognizable by collectors. Although many made in Gainesville or Pauls Valley are not stamped, those which are stamped generally carry MCCHESNEY in large letters inside the heel band. Some spurs of the McChesney styles have only a small arm and hammer symbol, which was also a trademark of the August Buermann Company, stamped on the heel band by the button. Some identi-

Unmarked McChesney spurs and matching bits with cut-out rattlesnake design in the heel bands of spurs and cheek pieces of bits. Silver and brass overlay. The Huber Collection has the same style without cut-outs. *Wheat Collection.*

Stamped MCCHESNEY in small letters under the outside buttons. Made by Nocona Boot Company between 1928 and 1933. They are half-mounted with silver on shank tips, buttons, and oblong circle and engraved shield on either side on outside heel bands. The spurs are plated and have swinging buttons. *Huff Collection.*

fying features of McChesney spurs include oblong buttons and silver mountings (called peanuts by collectors), mountings of silver and copper in a shield design, the chestnut bud and prairie tulip, a rectangle with indented sides and ends, V-shaped mountings on the inside of the heel bands, and a rectangular mounting with a spade at each end, seen mostly on gal-legs.[25] Kirby McPherson remembered seeing Mc-Chesney gal-legs with and without rowels, both at the Gainesville shop and in the collection of Capt. Tom Hickman, the famous Texas Ranger from that town.[26]

As stated in the Nocona catalog when it first announced the boot company's acquisition of the bit and spur business, "Mr. McChesney, who originated hand-forged bits and spurs of one-piece steel, was satisfied only with the best." That statement is a fitting epitaph.

Chapter 6

P. M. Kelly Looks Back

I don't care to be recognized as a successful businessman. I liked
mechanical work, and I just worked at my trade of bit and spur
making as a pleasure more than anything else. Whether I was
making money out of it or not was second consideration. My wife,
Hettie, figured that I ought to put a little more stress on being a
businessman. But you know, she couldn't take a country boy
and put him in town and make a financier out of him
right off the reel! —P. M. Kelly

Pascal Moreland Kelly was born to Clara and Richard S. Kelly in Van Zandt County, Texas, in 1886. His father, a schoolteacher, changed schools often when young Kelly was growing up, teaching at Sterling City, San Angelo, and Eden, Texas. One of Pascal's earliest recollections was of watching cattle herds being driven north up the trail that passed by Eden.[1] For him the jingle of the cowboys' spurs was a portent of things to come.

The Kelly family moved to Childress County, and when land in Beaver County, Oklahoma Territory, was opened for settlement, Richard Kelly filed on a quarter-section there. He had to be on the land within six months of filing or forfeit his right to homestead, so he sent Pascal, the oldest of three boys, ahead with the family while he himself remained behind to earn enough money from teaching to tide them over until their new home was established.

"We had a good team of horses and a mule," Kelly later recalled, "so in February of 1904 I took Mother, my brothers and sisters, and a minimum of household goods to the homestead. I was just a month short of being eighteen years old. Dad had built a little wooden building on the land to signify that he had put some improvement on his claim after he filed on it. When we got there, I dug a dugout. In the meantime, we stayed in that little wooden house and in the wagon.

"After we moved out of the little building, it was my first shop. I had picked up some buggy steel at Miami, Texas, where we crossed the Canadian River, and I bought a Sears and Roebuck bellows and an anvil and set up a blacksmith shop and went to making spurs. By the time I had outgrown that shop, I had made a little money, so I put up a pretty good sized building for a shop."[2]

Kelly had made his first spurs in 1903 in Childress, where the Kellys had rented a farm from Arthur Foster, who was away working at Spindletop. Foster also had a blacksmith shop and was a pretty good mechanic and silversmith, who could repair a gun stock or make a nice pair of spurs. "Foster let me have access to his shop," Kelly recalled. "I made my first spurs in that blacksmith shop when I was seventeen years old. They were just plain. I didn't mount them at the time, because I didn't know how to stick that mounting on. I went into Childress and learned from a tinner what kind of acid to use in order to make nickel silver solder adhere to the steel, and I couldn't wait to get home to experiment with it and mount those spurs. It wasn't long after that until we moved to Beaver County, and I was all set to go into business making spurs."

Several of the local cowboys wanted that first pair of spurs, so Kelly decided to raffle them off. "That brought me a little more money than they would have if I had sold them outright," Kelly said. "I put the money back into materials in order to make spurs." Kelly soon could sell spurs as fast as he could make them. At first to make a plain pair of spurs was a good day's work, and he could sell them for $4.00 to $4.50. Pascal's younger sister Lillian began pumping the bellows and handing him tools, and he soon was able to make a pair of spurs in half a day. "I could make $8.00 a day, and that sure beat $1.00-a-day cowboy wages! There wasn't anybody in that section of the country making the kind of money I was."

When Kelly heard of the 1904 Exposition in Saint Louis, he began saving his spur money to go. That fall a rancher named Hancock from Hansford County came by the place with a herd of big steers he was shipping to Kansas City from nearby Guymon, and Kelly hired on to accompany them. He delivered the cattle and bought a ticket on the Wabash to Saint Louis and the World's Fair, where he spent most of his time in the machinery building.

For a while after that he just traveled around. When he would get low on money, he would go back to his anvil and spur making and soon have another road stake. Kelly continued to sell all the spurs he could make. If he didn't have his own orders to fill, the hardware people in Guymon took every available pair.

"I started with only a pattern or two," Kelly said, "and then I began to add to them as I learned more about forging and handling the tools and shaping them up different. I began with just a simple spur with a straight shank, either mounted or plain. I didn't mark my first spurs, but it wasn't very long until I got a steel stamp, and I stamped KELLY BROS on them toward the end of the band under the button. That was the only place I ever marked my spurs. My brothers, Grady and Leo, were in school, and I figured that when they got older, they could come in the shop with me, and the business would already be established as Kelly Brothers."[3]

Kelly drifted around and sporadically made spurs back at the home place until 1907, when the money panic hit and times were suddenly hard. There was a lot of freighting from Hansford County in northern Texas into Indian Territory, and the freight wagons passed the Kelly place. Everything was hauled by wagons and teams, and the horses had to be shod regularly. Lon Hayes, who ran a livery stable in Hansford, asked Kelly to move to Hansford and put in a shop. He promised to give Kelly enough horseshoeing to keep him going no matter how other business went. That sounded pretty good to Pascal, so he moved his tools to Hansford in 1907.[4]

P. M. Kelly stands in the door of his shop in Hansford, Texas, which he operated from 1907 until 1910, when he went to work for McChesney in Paul's Valley, Oklahoma. *Photo from* Western Horseman, *Courtesy P. M. Kelly.*

There, a man who worked for Swift Packing Company told Kelly he would put up a good blacksmith shop and rent it to Kelly cheap. Pascal agreed. The blacksmith was the town mechanic in those days, and Kelly did all kinds of blacksmith work as well as making spurs.

"Those boys down on the Canadian River toward Childress got to sending me orders for spurs through one of the cowboys, who became my agent," Kelly recalled. "He would come to Hansford and turn in his spur orders, but I also developed a good business from the other blacksmithing. Soon I had more work in the blacksmith shop than I could do, but I told a committee of citizens that I believed I'd quit blacksmithing and just make spurs." They protested, arguing that cow business was a thing of the past, and spur making a dead duck.

Kelly had made his decision, however, so he wrote to J. R. McChesney, the leading spur maker west of the Mississippi. He had visited McChesney's plant in Gainesville in 1907, and McChesney had offered him a job then. Kelly now decided to accept his offer. He had bought spurs from McChesney to help fill his own orders. "I sold his spurs just as they were. I don't remember that they even had his stamp on them. In fact, I don't think that he put his name on his spurs at all when I worked for him. When I decided to make spurs full time, I thought, 'McChesney's got the best set-up in the country, and that's the best place to get more experience.' So I wrote him a letter. This was 1910, and he had moved from Gainesville to Pauls Valley, Okla-

Stamped KELLY BROS under regular swinging buttons of both spurs. Pictured in Kelly Brothers Catalog no. 17, Dalhart, Texas (circa 1917) as No. 74 Spur. Made with ⅞-inch band only, plain, mounted one side or both with silver leaf on heel bands, silver heart button, and silver rowel pin cover. Pictured is a single-mounted pair with original rowels. *Huff Collection; photo by Bob L. Trantham.*

homa. He wrote me back, 'You can go to work any day you come.'" So Kelly hired on.

He worked with McChesney for nine months, getting good wages from the day he joined the shop. McChesney began to keep Kelly in the machine shop making dies and tools as his right-hand man. Kelly was soon spending all his spare time working on gasoline and steam engines. He was so busy he soon had another fellow from McChesney's shop, Clyde Parker, helping him. McChesney and Kelly worked well together, and his apprenticeship was well spent.

In 1911 Kelly decided to go into business for himself in Dalhart. He bought an unfinished punch press casting from McChesney and shipped it to Dalhart. He got acquainted with the man running the Dalhart machine shop, and by using the lathe and shaper and tools at the town garage, he finished making his equipment. He bought flywheels, made the crankshafts and clutch, and soon had the punch press going. Then he was ready to make dies and punch spur rowels.

"Before then," Kelly said, "I had to saw the teeth in the rowels. To take a hacksaw and make a pair of rowels was almost a day's work, but once I could blank one out to shape, I could finish the rowels right quick! The next thing I had to make was a roller mill to roll the bands instead of hammering them. I got a five-inch steel railroad axle and cut it in two pieces about six or seven inches long to make a roller, and I got a big gasoline engine flywheel to drive the shaft. I didn't care whether business was very good yet or not, because I wanted time to be making tools that could cut down on the handwork. As quick as I was making enough money to hire another boy or two to help do the work, I kept enough forgings ahead for them to work on, and I put in my time making tools."

When Kelly went to Dalhart, his main objectives were getting his business going and making spurs. Once he had made enough equipment to get his spur business in operation, he decided that if a man was a designer who could make things, there was a good market for other products, like gasoline engines. All big ranches in West Texas pumped water with open-crankcase engines. Because of the dust storms, they needed closed crankcases. Kelly designed an oil engine, and these too he sold as fast as he could finish them. Later, though, he admitted, "I had tackled a million-dollar proposition when I didn't have finances to put up a popcorn stand."

Once Kelly was established, he needed help with his spur business. He corresponded with Clyde Parker, who had been a foundryman before going to work for McChesney. He was getting only about $2 a day at McChesney's and Kelly offered him $5 a day. Accepting, he moved to Dalhart in 1912 or 1913. He put $250 into the business and joined Kelly as a partner, and the business became Kelly Brothers and Parker. "When Clyde became my partner, my brothers were too young to be considered responsible men for carrying on the business, and Parker was a man about my age or maybe a year older. Clyde relieved me of seeing to the production. I was making machines and tools, and I'd explain to Clyde how one operated and then he'd train the other boys to operate it. He kept production coming along. Any time I added a machine to speed things up, he'd adapt to it, and we both profited by it. Clyde was due a lot of credit for my early success. It was teamwork. When Parker came in with me, we stamped our spurs KB&P or KELLY BROS. & PARKER until the partnership was dissolved in 1919."

Several of McChesney's best workers went with Parker to Dalhart. "I didn't mean to be taking Mac's men," Kelly later said, "because Mac and I were good friends, but I paid more money, and they came. I had some men who had worked for him for more than ten years. . . . While we were in Dalhart, I obtained a patent in 1921 on a riveted swinging button that I used for a number of years. I also made just the regular swinging button and the stationary button on the turned-up heel band.[5] I finally quit making my patented button, because I could make the staple button faster, and the staple was accepted just about as well. The one I had patented consisted of a little piece the swinger went around that was blanked out with a die. The button was put on the strap, and the last step was to attach the whole assembly to the spur band with two little rivets. It was more of a job, so I charged a dollar extra for them. I began making these buttons about 1917 or 1918 and continued them for a long time."

Bits were cut out with a die, too. Kelly had made a few bits at Hansford, but he did not get into bits to any extent until he opened his shop at Dalhart. In the beginning they were all one-piece. About the time he started his assembly-line process for making spurs in El Paso, he began welding bits to see how that would be accepted. Kelly did such a good job welding them that there was no problem, and he eventually made only welded bits.

"When we first went to making bits and spurs," Kelly recalled, "we sold about two pair of spurs to one bit. Through the years, there would occasionally be some feature about a bit that I'd follow a suggestion, but 90 percent of them would be my own designs. Laymen don't know what is practical and can be made with a die and what can't."

The old Chihuahua spur was at one time, as one of Kelly's mechanics said, "as standard as Cream of Wheat." E. T. Amonett, who sold Chihuahua spurs he bought in Mexico at his main store in Roswell, New Mexico, encouraged Kelly to make Chihuahuas. About 1917 he made dies and tools to do so, and this style was then a leader for years. Porter in Phoenix sold hundreds of them, but almost overnight the Chihauhua spur lost its popularity. By 1939, Kelly said, "the Chihuahua fad had died down to where I discontinued it."[6]

Times had gotten pretty hard, and the spur business had its ups and downs, especially when certain sections of the country were drought stricken. If a spur manufacturer wasn't operating over a pretty big territory through jobbers, sales were small. Kelly sold through Schoellkopf in Dallas, Padgitt and Al Franks in San Antonio, Straus-Budenheimer in Houston, jobbers up through Lincoln, Nebraska, and Dodge and Fisher Brockman in Minneapolis, Minnesota. Kelly had been working through jobbers since not long after he went to Dalhart in 1911.[7]

When World War I began, the army took seven men out of Kelly's plant, including his head machinist, a little Frenchman named Roy Deruen. The war also made it difficult to get materials, so Clyde and Pascal, too old for the draft, decided that one should volunteer to work for the government and the other would handle the business. It was agreed that Kelly would go. He took a blacksmith named Pettijohn and drove to California, where they went to work for Bethlehem Steel as machinists in the Oakland shipyards. After the Armistice was signed, Kelly returned to Texas. Pettijohn stayed in California, where he and Parker decided to open a spur factory. Kelly bought Parker out, and Parker joined Pettijohn in Los Angeles. But Parker died from a heart attack before the spur shop ever opened. Kelly, who had stayed in Dalhart, took over the shop there.

The change did not interfere with anything, Kelly said. "I went back to stamping the spurs KELLY BROS. When Parker and I were stamping spurs KELLY BROS. & PARKER or KB&P, we stamped the bits that way, too. . . . Then after 1939 when my brothers were out of the company, we just used KELLY, even though all of the literature read P. M. Kelly & Sons."[8]

In 1918, Pascal married Hettie Vititoe, an Indiana girl who was teaching school in Texhoma, Oklahoma. Their first son, Bob, was born late in 1919, and their oldest daughter, Helen Margaret, a little over a year later. Next came Mary Louise and Jack. After Kelly moved the business to El Paso in 1925. Hettie worked in the office and took an active part in the company.[9]

All the time Kelly was making spurs, he was also making oil engines. "I was bleeding the spur business to death furnishing the finances to develop the engines," he remarked. "I had those 'Kelly Hot Ball Engines' scattered out all over that Plains country."[10] Word even got into Denver that any cowboy could run one, and A. E. Bent, who was head of the Denver Power and Light Company, heard about it and financed Kelly. At Bent's suggestion, Kelly took the engine to the oil fields and was soon flooded with orders. About that time Bent died of a heart attack, and Kelly borrowed money and bought Bent's part of the engine business from his son.

"I needed to get to a larger city where labor was more plentiful than in Dalhart," he said. "El Paso would be nearer the foundries and labor. I had stayed in Dalhart for fourteen years. I went to El Paso and went to finishing the rest of my engines. I was shipping them right and left and had more castings ordered when the 1929 Depression hit and knocked the bottom out of everything. Things quietened down to where we couldn't sell an engine or anything else. That stopped the work."

In Dalhart, Kelly had employed eighteen men making spurs in his shop on Denrock Avenue. His engine shop and spur shop were in the same building, separated by a partition. Only seven men moved to El Paso with him. One was J. R. Barker, who had worked earlier at McChesney's in Pauls Valley and who continued to

Kelly in his El Paso office. *Photo by Jack Kelly.*

work for Kelly until he retired. Another was Clyde Box, who worked for him for thirty years.

Kelly discontinued shipping through the jobbers during the Depression. He had allowed the jobbers 40 percent discounts and dealers 25 percent. "The jobbers built me, and they nearly broke me," Kelly said. "When the slump came, the traveling men couldn't write business enough to justify keeping them on the road, and they pulled them off. That killed my business." So Kelly wrote Hartman

Stamped KELLY BROS under patented button swinger on both spurs. Large silver buttons and mounted with silver V's along heel band and shank. Available plain or mounted one side or both sides. Original star rowels. One-inch heel band only. This bronc spur is pictured in Kelly Brothers Catalog no. 20, El Paso, as "No. 183—Paddy Ryan Special" and is marked KELLY BROS in heel band. Crockett Catalog no. 12, Kansas City, Missouri, pictures the same spur, No. 183, "The Paddy Ryan." *Wheat Collection.*

Brothers, jobbers in Lincoln, Nebraska, saying "I can sell a few spurs to the dealers C.O.D., enough to kind of stay in business." One of the Hartman brothers replied, "Kelly, we're all in the same boat. I wouldn't hesitate a minute to sell to anybody I could, any way I could. You've got our consent to go direct to the dealers." Kelly began selling spurs that way, but times were still hard.

In the mid-1930s an official in the Mexican Ministry of Agriculture came to El Paso with plans for opening a pumping business across the river in the Rio Grande Valley. He needed engines and offered both to move Kelly's shop and to finance everything if he would move to Mexico City to build them. He offered Kelly a salary in American money, much more than he was making in his shop at that time. Kelly had two brothers who could run the El Paso shop, so he agreed. Kelly and his family went to Mexico in 1935 and stayed until the end of 1939.

When Kelly returned to El Paso, he found that the spur business was pretty quiet, so he bought his brothers out and soon got back in harness. He wanted just enough business to live on while he made tools to speed things up once he got back into full operation. His tool and die work and experience in building machines soon put him ahead of others in the spur business.

About that time there was a changeover in spurs. Cowboys on ranches used a long-shank spur, but rodeo hands, who constituted his new market, used one with a short shank. It took a redesign of the spurs in order to fit the market, and that called for new dies. Kelly worked day and night until he got his business going again. "When I came back to El Paso from Mexico, I began to drop the older, long-shank spurs that had been good sellers but were dying out. When I would add a new design, I would discontinue an old one, because trying to carry too many designs required too

Made by P. M. Kelly & Sons, stamped KELLY on heel bands of both spurs. Mounted with gold dragons set with green gems for eyes and red gems along body and tail. Mounted on tapered heel bands facing the shanks. Large coins are on the buttons and small coins cover the rowel pins. *Huff Collection; photo by Bob L. Trantham.*

much tied up in inventory. I went to work redesigning, and I developed styles of spurs and named them after prominent rodeo cowboys. They just went like wildfire. We had the Booger Red, the Jerry Ambler, the Bud Linderman, the Jim Shoulders and the Toots Mansfield. . . . With new designs in the early 1940s, I began to gain ground, and the business was just growing every day. I also offered a cheaper line of spurs, which were stamped RODEO.[11]

"Salesmen would carry pairs of our spurs as samples until they got to selling the pairs and not turning the money in, and they'd run out of samples, so after I came out of Mexico, I only let my salesmen have singles. They couldn't sell one spur very easily."

After World War II, Kelly's son Bob, who was a cost production engineer in a steel mill in Gary, Indiana, joined his father as a full partner and took over the office. "I had this spur business on its feet, but I could still push it faster and further if I didn't have to split my attention between the office and the shop," Pascal noted. "With Bob's help, we began to gain fast, and I made more money and progress the last fifteen years I was in business than I had all the rest of my life."[12]

Kelly's company was sold to Jim Renalde in 1965.[13] "Business was better than ever," Pascal observed, "but I was getting older every day. We were making good progress and had put up a nice building. We had taken on a number of jobbing lines like Bona Allen's saddle blankets, and we did $100,000 worth of business on boots alone one fall. Renalde had been trying to buy us out for some time. He had already bought the Crockett business. I told Bob, 'Right now we are in good shape to sell out. Get hold of Jim Renalde and ask him if he's still interested.'

"Renalde said, 'We'll buy any day that you want to sell.' So Bob made an appointment, and the old James Renalde and his son, young Jim, and J. G. Hoagland, who was his main mechanic and vice-president of production, came to El Paso. Hoagland had worked for Renalde for twenty years in his brass foundry. It is

P. M.
Kelly

59

said he was the brains of the Crockett-Renalde Bit and Spur Shop. An agreement was reached, and Renalde bought out the shop and patents.

"When I sold out to Renalde," Kelly continued, "just one man who worked for me went to work for Crockett-Renalde. If he had taken two or three of my men with him, he would have been better off, because I was performing operations that were ahead of Renalde's methods. They looked at my methods, and then they took the equipment they wanted. There were some things that they should have taken that they didn't. I had seven tumbling barrels running, and some of those barrels were representing ten men's work. A barrel would run night and day, and it was always ready to work, where men had slow periods. I was doing the work, and the barrel did the finishing on spurs that you couldn't possibly do by hand without a lot of hand-work, and that was prohibitive because of the labor. Yet they were kind of staying with that handwork. I told them, 'I don't believe you're ever going to duplicate our goods until you go to tumbling and grinding them and deburring them like I'm doing right here in my barrels.' These were ball barrels, and I had invented something that the ball barrel people who made the steel balls in Hartford, Connecticut, had never gotten wise to. I made a way of cleaning the balls. When the balls got dirty and gummy, they wouldn't polish, so I made a way of cleaning them that I tried to get a patent on. It was turned down, because there was the same kind of operation on a tumbling barrel for cleaning oranges down in Florida. That barred my patent, but I adopted the method. [14]

"I had several machines in my shop that their tool maker himself looked at and didn't know what they were for. When I showed him how they worked, he grabbed them up. Yet he left some that he should have taken. But Hoagland took all of the dies, some that we had used since 1920.

"We owned the property that our big building was on, and we had bought the adjacent property. It had a five-room house on it that we used as a storeroom to put supplies in. I put an industrial steel fence around the yard and moved what was left out into that yard before we sold the building. I had some punch presses and a lot of equipment that Renalde already had, and they didn't need them, so I had a yard full of machinery. We sold the building and all the equipment in sixty days. Some of it went to Guadalajara, Mexico, some to Amarillo, some to Phoenix, Arizona, and the rest just scattered all over the country.

"Our business in El Paso hadn't stayed in one location the whole time. We had built a new shop at 1220 Myrtle Avenue during the last few years. Originally, the shop was on the corner of Cotton and Missouri." [15]

The last few years of Pascal Kelly's life he lived in Oceanside, California, with his son, Jack. He could recall names and dates, spur styles and customers with amazing clarity. When P. M. Kelly died on March 10, 1976, the West lost not only a fine artist, whose name represented quality in bit and spur manufacturing, but a man of integrity. As his wife wrote, "He deserves credit in many ways and for a life above reproach, the result of being reared by noble and honest parents." [16]

Chapter 7

Oscar Crockett and the Crockett Bit & Spur Company

McChesney had died and Kelly was in Mexico during the 1930s, the years that Oscar Crockett was expanding the Crockett Bit & Spur Company in Lenexa, Kansas, prior to his move to Boulder, Colorado, where the business reached its largest growth, employing 125 men. Crockett had begun as a country blacksmith; at his death in 1949, his company was recognized as a leader in its field.

Oscar Crockett was born November 27, 1887, in Pecos, Texas, where he spent his early years. His father, J. B. Crockett, was a stockman who traded in cattle and horses, so Oscar and his older brother, Arthur, grew up on the move. Much of West Texas was open land at that time; the Crockett family often lived out of a wagon, moving to where the trading was most profitable. [1]

"During my boyhood, my brother Arthur Crockett, was a spur maker, and it always interested me to watch him," Oscar wrote. No spurs have been found with Arthur's name on them, but the O. CROCKETT stamped on some old Crockett spurs might have been to differentiate between Oscar's and Arthur's work. Hazel A. Crockett, Oscar's widow, recalled that Oscar said he made his first spurs "in the shade of a tree." There is no evidence that Arthur Crockett, who was killed in an automobile accident in Texas about 1927, ever entered Oscar's bit and spur business. [2]

When Oscar went to Kansas City with a trainload of cattle from Magdalena, New Mexico, in 1910, he decided to stay and soon had work at a blacksmith shop. "I made wagons during the day and worked on my own hook making spurs and bits at night," he wrote. "Soon I had enough money to open a small shop of my own, and I went to Pawhuska, Oklahoma, in 1916." [3]

That venture was short-lived. In 1916 Crockett sold out and went to Bremerton, Washington, to work in the government shipyards. When the Armistice ended World War I, Oscar returned to Kansas City and presumably opened another shop. However, he soon went to work for the Charles P. Shipley Saddlery & Mercantile Company. [4] On the heel bands of many of the Crockett styles in Shipley Catalog no. 16, published about 1917, are the initials C&G, perhaps Crockett and a partner. [5]

Crockett worked for Shipley until January, 1920, when, with the financial aid of his uncle, W. Brice Crockett, he bought the bit and spur segment of the Shipley business and set up shop across the street. The Crockett Bit & Spur Company at 1525 Genesee Street had a factory in the back and a retail store at the front. Crockett's

Texan Oscar Crockett bought Shipley's shop in Kansas City, Missouri, in the early 1920s, and the Crockett Bit & Spur Company soon became a leader in the field. *Courtesy Hazel Crockett.*

Catalog no. 7 listed the firm's address as 1602 West 16th Street, but Catalog no. 12, sent out in 1932, showed the business back on Genesee Street. Oscar's father and uncle peddled his spurs and bits across the country, and his business grew until he had eight or ten men working for him.[6]

Oscar Crockett began distributing catalogs of his products when he acquired the Shipley spur business. In 1940 an illustration in Catalog no. 14 showed a plant in Lenexa of over 5,000 square feet, with eighteen employees, 177 styles of spurs, 105 bits, and a patented honda (for lariats) developed by Crockett. He advertised that for a "modest additional charge" all of his Tool Steel bits and spurs could be ordered in a

Stamped O. CROCKETT inside heel band. Swinging buttons and sixteen-point rowels. Silver overlay with cut-outs in the mounting on heel bands. Pictured in Catalog no. 3 (1927) of Duhamel Company, Rapid City, South Dakota. Called "The Roy Quick" No. 163 Spur in Crockett Catalog no. 12, Kansas City, Missouri. *Huff Collection.*

chromium-plated finish, but he did not guarantee the products to be absolutely rust proof or peel proof. As P. M. Kelly remarked, Wallie Boone of San Angelo, Texas, had put all of them to plating spurs.

In Catalog no. 12 (1932), spurs were priced from $3.50 to $25.00 a pair. They could be ordered single-mounted or, for $1.00 to $3.00 more, double-mounted. Crockett had several spur styles that continued in popularity and appeared continuously in his catalogs, styles such as the Johnny Mullins and the Paddy Ryan. The only change in them was that when the business was in Boulder, Colorado, the spurs were made of stainless steel.[7]

Crockett spurs and bits were also advertised in saddle shop catalogs such as those of Miles City Saddlery; the Denver Dry Goods Company; Otto F. Ernst, Inc., of Sheridan, Wyoming; Hamley & Co. of Pendleton, Oregon; and the Duhamel Company of Rapid City, South Dakota. Crockett made a stylish but durable product that was well accepted by horsemen in all parts of the country.

About 1930 Oscar expanded his business in Kansas City by offering hand-made boots to his customers. He hired a bootmaker, but that line of work proved not to pay and was soon dropped.[8] Oscar and Hazel Crockett were married in 1932. Shortly after their marriage, they bought land near Lenexa, Kansas, and moved the factory there. "We had 240 acres on one side of the road where the shop was, and 40 acres on the other side of the road, where we later built a new house and where I had my milk cows and chickens," Hazel remembered. "The business grew, and we built on to the factory, and in 1939 I saw to the building of a new house."[9]

Oscar
Crockett

63

About 1932 Oscar Crockett moved his bit and spur business to a site near Lenexa, Kansas, where he employed fourteen workers. *Courtesy Hazel Crockett.*

Crockett Bit & Spur company took on new lines. Hazel recalls delivering a silver-mounted martingale to a man in Enid, Oklahoma, so that he would have it in time to use in a parade. That was personalized service. Oscar hired an engraver from Wisconsin to make belt buckles, which also became a popular line. The Crockett Bit & Spur Company was booming. "When we'd get behind," Mrs. Crockett continued, "I'd go back over to the shop at night and help Oscar make buttons. I never did that after we moved to Boulder, because we had plenty of help then. Oscar could do anything there was to do in the way of making spurs, other than he didn't claim to be an engraver. He worked three engravers while we were in Lenexa. Even after we moved to Boulder, he dressed so that he could meet the public, but if there was anything that needed to be fixed, he'd roll up his sleeves and go back in the shop and show the man how to do it. The steel spurs were always mostly handwork, and Oscar took pride in the workmanship. When he took on an aluminum line of bits and spurs, of course they were cut out by machine or extruded, but the engraving and a lot of the work was still done by hand." [10]

With the demand for aluminum products, Crockett entered into that phase also, but he continued his steel lines. "You see, aluminum is not nearly as strong as steel, but Oscar guaranteed everything that he made," Mrs. Crockett pointed out. "There was quite a demand for aluminum, but as far as value was concerned, steel was much more in demand." Catalog no. 29 of the N. Porter Company of Phoenix, Arizona, pictures Crockett spurs, all steel, but in Porter's 1941 Catalog no. 32 there

Stamped CROCKETT inside both heel bands. Gal-leg style made of nickel or Airplane Metal with silver mounting. Eight-point rowels. *Wheat Collection.*

are Crockett Never-Rust Silver Steel spurs, hand-forged tool steel spurs, and aluminum spurs, which are referred to as being made of Airplane Metal.[11]

When the United States entered World War II, Crockett began having trouble getting help in Lenexa. The young men of the area were either drafted or went into farming or defense work. Oscar and Hazel had made a number of business trips to Colorado and liked the climate, so they decided to look into the possibilities there. After visiting several towns, Crockett was in the Miller Stockman store in Denver one day when a salesman asked, "Why don't you look at Boulder? You might like it." The Crocketts drove to Boulder and within two hours had leased a building. They leased out their farm near Lenexa and moved eight of their workers, several truck loads of steel, and their shop—the whole kit and caboodle—to Colorado in 1943. A couple of the men did not stay long, but Oscar had no trouble getting more help. He had never hired older men before, but he found plenty of capable older help in Boulder, men who did not want to drive back and forth to work in a Denver defense plant. Boulder was a small town at that time, and the Crockett Company was only its second manufacturing company. Business mushroomed, and even though he had no government contracts during the war, Crockett was soon operating with a full head of steam and 125 men. He had only one salesman, a man named Ashbaugh, and sold most of his spurs through jobbers and by mail order.[12] His products, stamped CROCKETT, soon sold throughout the world, and he had dealers in all forty-eight states.

As long as Oscar Crockett was in the bit and spur business, he stayed in touch with the users of his products and was liked by them. He enjoyed going to the rodeos and jawing with the cowboys, taking orders and getting new ideas. Two things he would refuse to make were severe spade bits and sharp-roweled spurs. "When Oscar would get a good suggestion for a new spur or bit from some cowboy, he'd go home

Stamped CROCKETT. Staples for swinging buttons set in middle of wide heel band. Silver mounting on shank tips, bars on heel bands and on buttons. Brass flying eagle on outside bands. This style was made with and without chap guards and with a variety of decorations. Pictured on title page of Crockett Catalog no. 11, Kansas City, Missouri, about 1928. Listed as No. 201 Spur. *Huff Collection; photo by Bob L. Trantham.*

and work it out," his wife recalled. "I can still see him and the bookkeeper standing there figuring out how much it would cost to produce, and Oscar could figure in his head faster than the bookkeeper could figure on paper, and he'd come up with the answer first."

"During World War II," she continued, "we never had much trouble getting steel, but we had trouble getting silver. We even made a trip to Ogden, Utah, once when Oscar heard about a place there where he could buy silver, but we couldn't get all we needed. We used a lot of Mexican silver there for a while, and it worked just fine."

When the man who had leased their Lenexa farm decided to move, the couple got to thinking of their happy times on the farm and decided to move back. They stayed in Kansas, returning to Colorado about every six weeks to check on the business. After a few such trips, Oscar decided to sell the company and retire to the farm, and he discussed a deal with several employees who wished to buy the company: Allen McGinnis, Joe Russell, Jack Randall, and Roy Webber. Until the details could be worked out, the Crockett Bit and Spur Company remained under the direction of its founder and the Crocketts continued to divide their time between Kansas and Colorado. On a business trip to Boulder in 1949, Oscar had a heart attack and died the next day. Hazel said, "Those last six months on the farm were the happiest we had spent."

At Oscar Crockett's death, his widow took up the reins of the business for a year and a half. The deal discussed by Oscar and his four prospective buyers was never finalized. "When James Renalde made me a good offer in 1951," Hazel later said, "I agreed to sell him the business. Oscar had worked so hard and been so proud of his company that I hated to see it go, but I felt that James Renalde would operate it properly." Renalde had started the Denver Metals Foundry in 1938 and made buckles and saddle hardware and aluminum bits and spurs. When the Crockett Bit & Spur Company was purchased by Renalde, it continued operation under the same name at the same location, 944 Pearl Street in Boulder, just west of the downtown area. In 1965 Renalde also bought the company of P. M. Kelly & Sons of El Paso, Texas, and moved it to Colorado. When James Renalde died in 1973, the combined businesses passed to his son, Jim Renalde, who undertook considerable automation and changed to making primarily steel items, discontinuing most aluminum products.[13] The company's catalog, which showed a spur rowel in place of the ampersand, was titled *Crockett and Kelly—Bits & Spurs by Renalde.*

After Crockett and Renalde merged, the spurs were stamped with a horseshoe CR symbol on the heel band or the button swinger. Prior to that, Crockett Bit & Spur Company had stamped CROCKETT in capital letters inside or on the top edge of the heel band.

Al Gabriella, who had become a Crockett employee when the business was first moved to Boulder, was still with the company as engraver after Renalde bought it. As he stood one day cutting wriggles and beautiful free-hand designs onto a spur's silver mounting, many examples of Crockett spurs with identifying order numbers on the heel bands hung on the wall beside him. "Many of those styles are obsolete, but I keep them for sentiment's sake," he said. "I enjoyed working for Mr. Crockett. He was a rough and ready sort and a good sport, and the shop had a homey feeling."[14]

So, in the end, McChesney was no more, and the Crockett and Kelly lines were no longer made by a Crockett or a Kelly, but had been combined as Renalde, Crockett & Kelly to become the world's largest bit and spur manufacturer of the late 1960s and 1970s.

In 1979 Jim Renalde sold the business, which was renamed Crockett & Kelly, Inc., and moved to Broomfield, Colorado.[15] By the mid-1980s the company had closed. Perhaps success depended on a Crockett or a Kelly or a Renalde, who understood the needs of horse people and could supply the goods they liked. The making of Crockett spurs had come a long way from the days when Oscar Crockett's forge glowed red-hot and the ring of his hammer drifted on the western breeze. His spurs, like their maker, are now part of our country's history.

Chapter 8

The Shops of Bischoff and Shipley

In various ways, McChesney provided the springboard for several other top spur makers: P. M. Kelly, G. A. Bischoff, Tom Johnson, Jr., Clyde Parker, and Charles P. Shipley. Kelly, Johnson, and Parker all worked for him in Pauls Valley. When McChesney moved there from Gainesville in 1910, some of his best hands stayed in Texas. Among them were an engraver, N. C. Browning, and McChesney's head forger, Albert Dickerman. McChesney's former employees joined a local businessman and blacksmith, George Andrew Bischoff, to form "G. A. Bischoff & Co., Manufacturers of High Grade Bits and Spurs." These men developed their own distinctive styles and did beautiful work.

G. A. Bischoff & Company

The Bischoff company issued Catalog no. 1 on September 1, 1911, picturing twenty-one styles of spurs and three bits. The bits and spurs were identified as "Style A," "Style B," and so on. Each style was available with eight to eleven different mountings. The Bischoff company was not geared for mass production, nor did it have the means to reach the public through jobbers as did Kelly and McChesney, so it remained in business for only a few years.[1] Some of the spurs were stamped GAB and some G. A. BISCHOFF & CO. inside the heel bands of both spurs. As Kelly remembered Bischoff and his shop, "he had a real good, high-class blacksmith shop. Bischoff made up some nice samples and brought them to West Texas. By that time, I had left McChesney and had things going pretty good at my shop in Dalhart, so I already had the business sewed up in that area. . . . Bischoff had a good product, but his problem was in production and distribution."[2]

George Bischoff was born at Emmettsburg, Maryland, on October 16, 1862, one of ten children of German-emigrant parents. George completed his apprenticeship at the Baker Carriage factory in 1881 at the age of nineteen and moved to Dallas, Texas. For the next several years, he worked as a carriage builder throughout the northern and western states. In the late 1880s, while visiting his parents in Florida, George met Mollie Jane Tucker of Dade City, whom he married on December 24, 1890.[3]

The Bischoffs and their two daughters., Gertrude and Cora Lee, moved to Gainesville in 1894. They also were to have a son, William G. Bischoff. In the 1895 Gainesville City Directory, Bischoff was listed as a general blacksmith, with his shop

G. A. Bischoff, 1892, Dade City, Florida. *Courtesy Paul J. Schad.*

Stamped G. A. BISCHOFF and HAND FORGED in heel band of both spurs. Fine engraving on full silver mounting. Note distinctive Bischoff attachment of gal-leg shanks to heel bands. This was continued on certain styles made by Chas. P. Shipley Company after it acquired the Bischoff Company in 1915. Style F in Bischoff Catalog no. 1, September 1, 1911; could be ordered plain, half-mounted, or full-mounted, in silver, gold, red bronze, yellow bronze, or rough (without patent finish). Came with ⅝-inch band, 2¼-inch shank, 1⅝-inch rowel. *Huff Collection; photo by Bob L. Trantham.*

at 108 South Dixon. He soon moved to a two-story brick building at the corner of Main and Rusk streets, where he added a good business as a carriage builder to his blacksmith work.[4] The building is still there, and his sign advertising wagons can be seen faintly on the bricks on the Main Street side.

Bischoff was also active in civic affairs. He was elected to the City Council in 1906 and during his three terms was one of the members instrumental in obtaining the city water works from private owners.

Clinton McPherson was a young man living in Gainesville during the years Bischoff had his carriage business on Rusk Street. "My brother, Matt, worked for Bischoff for a while, and I used to visit him there," he remembered. "The blacksmith shop was on the first floor. While Matt worked there, Bischoff had a contract with the county to shoe the mules that were used by convict labor to maintain the roads. These mules weighed about seventeen hundred pounds and stood sixteen hands tall. They were often mistreated by their handlers, so when they were brought into Bischoff's to be shod, they were mean and hard to handle. . . . I recall that Mr. Bischoff was a big, stout man. He was dark complected and wore a mustache and whiskers. Bischoff had another man of German descent, August W. Gerneth, who worked for him and also had his own shop on Main Street. He was a larger man than Bischoff and powerful. He could handle those mules!"[5]

Bischoff knew how to change with the times. He owned the first Maxwell automobile in town and opened the Maxwell agency in the Bischoff Building at Rusk and Main. In 1910, W. L. Greenhall, who had for many years been the MKT Railroad ticket agent in Gainesville, became Bischoff's partner in the automobile business, selling Overlands. It is surprising, in fact, that with his interest in automobiles, Bischoff went into the spur business.[6]

Stamped G. A. BISCHOFF & CO. in both heel bands. Style A in Bischoff Catalog no. 1 (1911). Band ⅜-inch wide; 1½-inch shank. Silver mounted but also made plain, rough, and in a variety of mountings. No. 10 steel rowels with the points filed off. *Huff Collection.*

George Bischoff, like many of the other spur makers, was an innovative craftsman. McPherson recalled that Bischoff made his daughter a chain-driven buggy powered by a gasoline engine. "That thing coughed and sputtered down the street and caused more runaways than anything," he said.[7]

Bischoff spurs are easily recognizable by their unique designs. One unusual feature of the shank on Bischoff's gal-leg spur is that it is set on the heel band at an angle, attached only at the top of the leg. The shank is short from the knee up, and the shapely leg is rounded. Another characteristic of Bischoff spurs is that the ends of the heel band often turn up and are somewhat concave in the back and then round out behind the buttons. Another Bischoff design features an odd flair at the rowell end of the shank, almost a bird's head in appearance but unlike McChesney's goose head or Kelly's eagles.[8]

In 1895 Gainesville had supported seven livery stables, seven wagon yards, and eleven blacksmith shops; there were 17,100 horses and 3,628 buggies and wagons rendered for taxes. In 1915 the last livery stable closed, and late that same year Bischoff sold his bit and spur business to Charles P. Shipley.[9] In 1916 he and his family moved to Kansas City, where he may have worked for Shipley for a while. The Bischoffs lived in Kansas City until 1926, and at least part of that time, Bischoff was employed by the Mason Campbell Manufacturing Company.

In 1926 the family moved to Oklahoma City, where George owned the Western Wheel and Body Works, manufactured drays, and made truck bodies for OK Transfer Company. His son William G. Bischoff worked with him, and his daughter Gertrude lived in Oklahoma City. When World War II began, Bischoff went to work for Douglas Aircraft Corporation in Tulsa as a tool and die maker. George was Douglas's oldest employee, and several newspaper and magazine feature stories were written about him because of his skill and the accuracy of his work.[10]

Bischoff's grandson, Paul Schad, recalled, "My grandfather was a wonderful mechanic and a fine man. He was six feet two inches tall and muscular. He was a righteous type of fellow. Even at eighty years, he was very erect. He walked down the street like a marine."[11] Bischoff remained with the aircraft business until four months before his death, when ill health forced him to retire. He died on May 13, 1944, and was buried in Gainesville. His wife, Mollie, died on October 14 of that year.[12]

Charles P. Shipley Saddlery and Mercantile Company

The Charles P. Shipley Saddlery and Mercantile Company of Kansas City was founded by Shipley, a harness maker, in August, 1885. Shipley was born in Wooster, Ohio, on October 27, 1864, and it was in Ohio that he learned the saddlery and harness trade. With capital of three hundred dollars, which he borrowed from a friend, he started his saddlery company at the mouth of the Kaw River, across from the Armour Packing Company, but by the turn of the century he had moved to larger quarters. In 1903, a flood almost put him out of business, but he recovered from that and moved for the second time. At his new location, he began branching out from being strictly a harness maker to the manufacture of boots, saddles and bridles, whips, and all kinds of leather goods.

In 1886, Shipley had married Cora May Hendrickson of Olathe, Kansas; three children were born to them. The second, Clyde L. Shipley, joined his father in the mercantile business, and the company's 1911 catalog pictures twenty-two-year-old Clyde as vice-president and sales manager.

Shipley incorporated the business in 1910 and built the three-story Shipley building at 17th and Genesee streets, opposite the Livestock Exchange Building. The company advertised itself as wholesale and retail manufacturers. As part of its continued expansion in late 1915 or early 1916, Shipley bought Bischoff's company in Texas and the Kansas City shop of Oscar Crockett and put in his own foundry for the making of bits and spurs. Charles P. Shipley II later explained that Crockett "was then an apprentice to the man who originally started the bit and spur business."[13]

According to P. M. Kelly, Bischoff wanted out of the spur business because of financial and distribution problems, and Shipley wanted in to spite McChesney. When Kelly worked for McChesney in Pauls Valley, Oklahoma, he knew McChesney's daughter Rosetta, called Dude. "Dude and I would go together a little, and she was pretty confidential in telling me about the orders they were getting and any problems they had, and I would listen with both ears. She worked in the office and sent out the statements. Shipley in Kansas City was a good customer and bought a lot from McChesney, but they had a disagreement over a bill. Shipley finally wrote, 'If you don't quit pressing me for money, I'm going to put in a spur factory myself!' Dude showed me that letter, and by jiminy, he finally did exactly that! He found out Bischoff's shop was for sale, and Shipley bought him out, and one or two of McChesney's ex-workers went up to work for him in Kansas City." Bischoff himself may have worked for Shipley for a while, since upon selling his spur business, Bischoff and his family moved to Kansas City. Shipley was well established in the saddlery and mercantile business, with a large local trade as well as catalog customers, but,

Charles P. Shipley, as he appeared in his company's Catalog no. 12 (1912).
Courtesy National Cowboy Hall of Fame.

Stamped C. P. SHIPLEY and KAN CITY MO. in heel band of each spur. Full-mounted with silver and copper. Same configuration as Style R in Bischoff Catalog no. 1, 1911. Listed in Shipley Catalog no. 16 as No. X19. *Huff Collection.*

Gal-leg bits and spurs stamped C. P. SHIPLEY and KAN CITY MO. inside heel bands of both spurs and on both cheek pieces of the bit. Silver and brass mounting. Engraved. *Wheat Collection.*

Shipley spur of Oscar Crockett styling. Silver-mounted with a bronze star on outside heel band. This spur with a chap guard, No. X35, is pictured in Shipley Catalog no. 16 and is stamped inside the heel band C&G. It came with either turned-up buttons or swinging buttons. *Mitchell Collection.*

according to Kelly, he did not know what he was getting into as far as the bit and spur business was concerned.[14]

The Shipley company in Kansas city issued new catalogs periodically. Prior to their own entry into the spur business, Shipley's small catalog of 1913 pictured Buermann's Star Brand bits and spurs and a McChesney gal-leg. Half-mounted with silver slippers, the gal-leg spurs sold for $3.75; full-mounted with silver slippers, they sold for $4.50; and the deluxe model, full-mounted with golden slippers, cost $5.50. In Catalog no. 16, issued about 1917, the following notice appeared:

> We take pleasure in presenting to you our Catalog No. 16 of Bits, Spurs
> & Stirrups, which we are now manufacturing, having recently purchased
> the plants of Oscar Crockett of Kansas City, and G. A. Bischoff & Co., of
> Gainesville, Texas.
>
> We use only the highest grade of steel, and we mount our goods in gold,
> silver, and two colors of bronze. They are beautifully and artistically
> engraved and are sure to please. You can make a razor of one of our bits or
> spurs and it will cut smooth and clean, because it is made of the right kind
> of stuff.

That catalog pictures forty-two styles of spurs and twelve bits. The spurs are two distinct types, Bischoff's and Crockett's. Some of the pictures of the Bischoff styles show G.A. BISCHOFF & CO. stamped inside the heel band, and several of the Crockett spurs and bits are stamped C&G. The spurs that were made in the Shipley shop were stamped C. P. SHIPLEY KANSAS CITY, MO. in capital letters inside the heel band. Catalog no. 17, published in 1918, shows these same C&G-stamped spurs plus some of the McChesney styles, but few Bischoff-type spurs. Perhaps Crockett had taken over the shop by then. Bischoff's spurs were trim, lightweight, and well made, and many of the early Shipley styles follow the Bischoff patterns. The heavier Shipleys have the Crockett flavor, as they naturally would after Oscar Crockett took over the Shipley shop.[15]

Shipley's Catalog no. 18 pictures Crockett-style spurs, the same ones that appear in a later Catalog no. 9 put out by Crockett Bit & Spur Company in the 1920s, when it was located at 1602 West 16th Street in Kansas City. In Shipley's Catalog no. 19, issued in 1923, there are still a few holdovers of the Bischoff style, but instead of the Crockett type, there are Buermann spurs with the Star Brand but advertised as "'Security' Steel Band Cowboy Spurs. Best Fitting and Strongest All-around Spur on the market." Catalog no. 27 continues to show these Star Brand spurs in 1933, and in the 50th Anniversary Catalog of 1935 there is a two-page spread of Buermann styles, which by then were made by North & Judd Company. There were also Crockett spurs and those designed by McChesney but made by Nocona Boot Company. The catalog states: "This page shows the general outline of the finest line of handmade spurs. We make them in our own shop. Any style made to order." This may indicate that the company bought unmarked spurs and sold them as its own, not an uncommon practice. By this time Shipley was apparently buying the finished product from Crockett, McChesney, and North & Judd, and was strictly a dealer.

Kelly once visited the Shipley shop while Oscar Crockett was head man. "The bit and spur factory was up on the third floor of the Shipley building when I visited Crockett there. Shipley didn't get to making very many more spurs than he sold, but he had a wonderful retail trade in Kansas City. The Stockyards were there, and cowboys from everywhere went into Kansas City, which was looked on as a big distribution point of western goods. They all bought from Shipley. That's how Shipley became so interested in making spurs. It wasn't long before he saw that it wasn't working out too good for him. Anybody in the bit and spur business has a lion by the tail! He has got to know what he's doing. If he has much overhead, the secret is production and distribution, and Shipley soon wanted out, just as Bischoff had.

"Oscar Crockett's uncle Brice told Oscar, 'I'll buy Shipley out if you want me to. You run the business and pay me as you can.' So Oscar took him up on it. They bought the tools from Shipley and moved right across the street and opened up under the name Crockett Bit & Spur Company."[16]

Perhaps the downfall of both Bischoff and Shipley as spur makers was caused by the lack of dealers to distribute and advertise their products elsewhere. Shipley's retail business was not sufficient to warrant maintaining a shop, and neither man's products were sold through other retail companies' catalogs, as were Kelly's, Crockett's, McChesney's, and Buermann's—all manufacturers who established ongoing businesses. Spur makers such as Bianchi, Bayers, and Bass enjoyed success without extensive retail arrangements, but they operated as individuals and did not have the overhead of supporting a number of employees. In spite of their lack of success as manufacturers, today spurs stamped SHIPLEY and BISCHOFF are much sought after by collectors.

Charles P. Shipley died in September of 1943. His son Clyde died in October, 1952, at which time Clyde's son, Charles P. Shipley II, took over the business and ran it until it closed in 1972. Shipley's was known for superior products, whether spurs

Made by Bob Boone. Unmarked; half-mounted with silver on outside of shank and cut-out button in shape of star. Silver plate on heel band engraved BRAZOS. Photo is of fine iron work on inside of spurs. Buttons only are silver overlay. *Huff Collection.*

Made by Bob Boone. Unmarked; exceptionally fine iron work of
cut-out design overlaid with silver and engraved. *Huff Collection.*

Made by J. R. McChesney. Unmarked; shank is goose neck, overlaid and engraved as feathers. Silver-overlaid wings mounted on heel bands. Stationary buttons on turned-up heel bands silver mounted. Same style made by Kelly Bros. & Parker. Ten-point rowel. *Huff Collection.*

Stamped G. A. BISCHOFF & CO. inside heel band of both spurs. Half-mounted. Long, pointed silver mounting with a dot at the end, typical of Bischoff spurs. Plain button on turned-up heel band. Copper overlay on typical Bischoff shank. *Huff Collection.*

Right spur only stamped NO. 43 MADE BY J. O. BASS TULIA TEX. Silver
overlay and heart-shaped swinging buttons. Six-point rowels. *Huff Collection*.

Unmarked McChesney spurs, decorated with silver half-moons and peacocks with feathers
spread. McChesney made these spurs while his shop was in Gainesville, Texas. Nocona Boot
Company, which bought his business, continued to make this style until 1933. *Huff Collection*.

Made by August Buermann. Star with B overstamped on A under outside button; PAT'D stamped in heel band. No. 1422 in Buermann Catalog no. 35 (1922). Half-mounted with engraved silver inlay on heel band and shank. Inside heel band incised and stamped HAND FORGED STEEL under button. *Huff Collection.*

Marked C. P. SHIPLEY   KAN CITY MO in heel band of both spurs. Half-mounted with copper and silver overlay. Turned-up heel bands; eight-point rowels. *Huff Collection.*

82

Marked KELLY BROS. across end of band on right spur and under button on left spur. Silver heart swinging button, scroll on band, and arrow on straight shank. Twelve-point rowels. *Huff Collection.*

Marked K.B.&P. under outside button of each spur. Gal-leg spurs with a chap guard with silver and brass overlay; 1½-inch ten-point rowels. *Huff Collection.*

Made by Adolph Bayers of Truscott, Texas. Stamped BAYERS and 500, the pattern number, on inside of left spur under button. Full silver mounting on stainless steel. The right spur is an unmarked copy of the Bayers spur made by Billy Klapper of Pampa, Texas, to replace a spur that was lost. Silver bars decorate the inside heel bands, and the name Skeeter, written in longhand, is mounted on the outside bands. *Dennis Collection*.

Stamped CROCKETT on heel bands of both spurs. Fully half-mounted with engraved silver. Initials H. L. engraved on large silver disk in center of outside heel band of both spurs. *Huff Collection*.

and bits or leather goods. They had made boots and saddles for many notable people, including Buffalo Bill Cody, Tom Mix, Buck Jones, Will Rogers, and Franklin D. Roosevelt. At the end of World War II, Texan Adm. Chester Nimitz stepped up into a Shipley saddle and took up the reins on a Shipley bridle as he rode a white horse down the streets of Tokyo.[17]

Chapter 9

Robert Lincoln Causey, First Blacksmith on the Llano Estacado

When Bob Causey was twelve years old, he might not have known what he wanted to do with his life, but he sure knew what he did *not* want to do. He did not want to be a farmer like his father. Young Bob was born in Kansas City, Missouri, on February 12, 1868, Abraham Lincoln's birthday, and named Robert Lincoln in the great man's honor. He was one of ten children born to G. W. and Mary Crowder Causey.[1] Two of his older brothers, Thomas L. Causey, better known as George, and John Vancleve Causey, had not wanted to farm either, and both had gone west.

By the 1870s the two Causeys were on the West Texas plains, where they joined in the near-extinction of the buffalo. The Causey brothers with their partner, Frank Lloyd, and their skinners killed seventy-five hundred buffalo in the winter of 1877 in Running Creek Draw along Yellow House Canyon near present-day Lubbock. Two years later the Causeys and Lloyd returned to the area and built an adobe house near a seep spring in order to have a base camp from which to follow the last remnants of the buffalo herds.

George Causey killed his last buffalo in 1882 at Clear Lake, near present-day Seminole, the last of forty thousand attributed to him. By this time other hide hunters had left the range and cattleman Jim Newman had decided that the Sweetwater country to the south was becoming too populated for his likes. He saw the potential of the sea of grass to the northwest as grazing land and realized that all it would take to control it was buying the water rights from the buffalo hunters. For sixty dollars he purchased their adobe house and the nearby spring and moved his DZ cattle onto the free state land—free, that is, until the state of Texas traded 3.05 million acres to the Capitol Syndicate of Chicago, Illinois, in exchange for building a red granite state house in Austin. The land became the XIT Ranch, the largest in America.

While still in Yellow House Canyon, George Causey had changed from buffalo hunter to cattleman. When Causey sold his water rights to Newman, he moved his stock west into New Mexico near the present town of Bronco and set about improving the water supply on the OHO Ranch. He learned that water was not far beneath the surface in that supposedly waterless plains country, making it possible to graze cattle where there was no natural surface water for miles. Windmills were to become monuments to that discovery.

The Littlefield Cattle Company bought the improved water rights from Causey and ran its LFD-branded cattle north of Roswell along the Pecos River. Causey moved south of the LFD drift fence and set about establishing his headquarters and rejuvenating the old JHB Connected Ranch and the 7HR Ranch, where he planned to run cattle and horses.[2]

Bob Causey had been too young to leave Missouri and go to the buffalo range with his brothers, but in 1880, when he was twelve years old, he borrowed five dollars from a neighbor and hid under a railroad bridge as his mother and father left home for the day in the buggy. He then boarded the west-bound train and rode as far as five dollars would take him. In a now-forgotten rail town in Indian Territory the boy got a job in a blacksmith shop, where he worked for his board and one dollar a week for the next four years. He saved his money and soon repaid his debt to the neighbor in Missouri. During those four years as an apprentice blacksmith, young Causey learned to forge the steel and handle the tools that would later earn him renown.[3] By 1884 he was ready to move west again, this time to his brother George's ranch in the area of Lovington, New Mexico.

Bob's knowledge of the blacksmith's trade was put to use during the building of the Causey ranch headquarters whenever metal work was needed. A story-and-a-half house was constructed of flat rocks and mud mortar, as were barns and corrals. Bob built a small blacksmith shop and brought a forge, bellows, anvil, and necessary tools from Midland, Texas, but he was kept busy with cowboy chores. His brother had lots of broncs to be broken and calves to be branded as well as equipment to be repaired.[4]

In the late 1880s the younger Causey decided it was time to go out on his own. The frontier cattle town of Odessa, Texas, seemed a likely place to set up a blacksmith shop. One of his sisters, Nellie Causey Whitlock, had been widowed, and she and her son came to live with Bob in Odessa so the youngster could go to school. Causey put his nephew, Vivian H. Whitlock, to work in the shop as his apprentice.[5] A fancy pair of shop-made spurs set a top hand apart from a greenhorn, and Bob Causey could hammer out some fancy espuelas. He could even deck out the cowboy's horse with a bit to match the spurs. The general blacksmithing work paid the bills in Odessa until Causey became established in his bit and spur business.

Bob Causey, often credited as the originator of the famous gal-leg spur, was certainly one of the early spur makers to capitalize on this design.[6] The shank of the spur was shaped like a woman's leg with the toe holding the rowel pin. The cheek-pieces on the matching bit were formed by the lady's leg with the toes holding the rein rings. The silver that Causey used on his spurs and bits came from Mexican coins he brought back from Ciudad Juárez, across the border from El Paso. Mexican coins had more silver in them than U.S. coins, so they were softer and easier to work.[7]

It is said that Bob Causey was the first blacksmith on the Llano Estacado. When he set up shop in Odessa, the town was little more than a water stop on the Texas & Pacific Railroad. It had few stores, a one-room schoolhouse, a post office, and, of course, a saloon. By 1891, when Ector County was organized, the town was named the county seat. G. I. McGonagill was elected sheriff, and Causey was constable.[8] The sheriff had two boys, Clay, then twelve years old, and Walter. Clay McGonagill was to become one of the greatest steer ropers of all time.

Bob Causey, wearing a leather apron, stands in front of his blacksmith shop in Eddy (Carlsbad), New Mexico, in 1900. The blacksmith's apprentice is his nephew, Vivian Whitlock. *Courtesy University of Oklahoma Press.*

In 1895 Bob Causey moved his shop to Eddy, New Mexico, which is now Carlsbad. That was in the big ranch country, and his talents as a smithy were much needed. While in Carlsbad, Bob met Martha Agnes Bogle, the daughter of Sam and Martha Bogle, who operated a rooming house there. Bob and Agnes were married on January 14, 1903. Their only child, a daughter named Mary, was born in 1904 in Roswell, where Causey had opened a blacksmith shop. An incurable wanderer, by 1906 he had moved to Artesia, New Mexico, and formed a partnership, Causey & Osborn, which advertised "General Blacksmithing and Wood Work." Mary Causey Anglin said, "Dad was a man who did like to get around. He next had a shop in Pendleton, Oregon, for awhile, and then we moved to Rupert, Idaho, where he opened a business, but it was too cold there. He came home one day and said we were going back to Carlsbad. Mama told him, 'So far, Mary has been to six schools. When we get back to Carlsbad, you find us a home. I'm going to stay put until Mary finishes school. If you want to travel around looking for a better place, you can go by yourself.' Dad opened his shop there, and we lived in Carlsbad until after I graduated from high school." [9]

Causey's business flourished in Carlsbad, and he hired a helper. There were wagons to repair and horses to shoe, and his spurs and bits were in great demand. Causey not only had an artistic flair with steel, but he was a painter and an accomplished wood worker, who laminated and polished fancy wooden card boxes, card

Made by Robert L. Causey for New Mexico rancher Lige Merchant at Causey's blacksmith shop in the 200 block of South Main in Carlsbad. Stamped R.L.C. on heel band of both spurs. *Courtesy City Museum of Carlsbad.*

tables, and poker chip racks. He also mounted buffalo horns and deer and antelope antlers. [10]

In the 1890s his old friends the McGonagills had left Odessa and begun ranching near Monument Springs in New Mexico. Like all who made a living in a saddle, they valued good horses, and they raised the Billy and Steel Dust strains. A contemporary of "Little Joe" Gardner, Ed Echols, and Ellison Carroll, Clay tossed a fast loop over the big cattle from Tuscon to Cheyenne and Calgary. That was back in the days when they roped four-year-old steers and tied them down from a hundred-foot score line. That took not only an experienced hand with a rope but a good horse, and Clay McGonagill was always well mounted. He tied down many a fast steer from his two top horses, Wolf and Rowdy, and he rode to those steers with Causey spurs on his heels, as did many other cowboys and ranchers in the West Texas–New Mexico area. Clay had Causey make him a pair of spurs inlaid with rubies. As Mary Anglin recalled, "My mother said that Dad often bought jewelry and used the colorful sets out of it to decorate his spurs." [11]

The cowboys around Carlsbad looked forward to Saturday nights at Sol Schoonover's saloon, when a pair of Causey spurs and often a matching bit were raffled off at a dollar a chance. Bob made a nice pocketful of jingles every week that way. [12]

Cowboys and ranchers came to Causey's shop for spurs and bits, and Bob also sold his wares at the local rodeos. He made a little glass exhibit case for them and carried it with him. Causey soon decided that he would make up spurs in advance, but not bits because every man had his own requirements for a bit. He made those on special order only and would also make spurs on order. Richard Merchant, world-champion calf roper of 1923 and one of the greatest cowboys of his day, ordered a pair of spurs with shanks made like the head and neck of a horse. Merchant wore those spurs when he participated in Tex Austin's rodeo in London in the 1920s. [13]

"My father had made spurs as long as I can recall," Mary Anglin said. "I remember seeing him take a bar of steel and split it to form the heel band. It was all handwork, including the rowels. He inlaid his spurs and bits using various metals,

Stamped with the maker's initials, R.L.C., under inside button on both spurs. Gal-leg design. Ends of turned-up heel bands angle slightly toward shank. Inlaid rowels and overlay filed down smooth on the edges with design incised in steel. Decorated less on insides of spurs. Saw-like rowels inlaid and incised. *Courtesy Mary Causey Anglin.*

but the spurs he made while in Carlsbad were fancier than his later spurs. He always marked his work RLC on the mouthpiece of each bit and by the inside button on each spur." [14]

By 1924 Bob Causey was ready to move again. A friend from Carlsbad had gone to Safford, Arizona, and wrote Bob enticing reports on the need for a blacksmith there, so the Causeys moved for the last time. Bob rented a large building in downtown Safford, but the owner of the utility company told him that the town's electricity lacked the power to operate his equipment. Causey was not one to be deterred; he took his Ford pickup and rigged it up with a belt running off a back wheel and powered his own equipment for about a year. Although Causey's spurs and bits were all hand work, which was time-consuming, he was inventive in making his own equipment in order to speed up his work. He had bought a large brick home on South First Street and put his blacksmith shop in an adobe building at one side of the house. He sent off for a gasoline motor, which he rigged up for his source of power in the new shop. [15]

Safford was in a farming area, so Causey sharpened plows and worked on farm equipment as well as making spurs and bits. When cowboys and ranchers passed through town, the Causey shop was a gathering place where old times, fast horses, and good ropers were recalled. "Dad was a quiet man who didn't have much to say except when his old friends came to visit," Mary Anglin remarked.

In 1932 he made a trip to California to see his brother, John, and the event was written up in a newspaper article in Pico, California, entitled "Buffalo Hunter Makes Welcome Visit to this Office." It reads in part:

> John Vancleve Causey of Inglewood, former famous buffalo hunter and
> acquaintance of Billy the Kid, and his brother "Bob" Causey of Safford,
> Arizona, visiting him after an absence of thirty years, paid the editor of this

Stamped R.L.C. under inside button on both spurs. Goose-head spurs with design incised around inlay on outside only of heel bands and shanks. Ends of turned-up heel bands angle slightly toward shank. Twenty-point rowels. *Courtesy Mary Causey Anglin.*

publication a visit the past week. . . .

Bob Causey brought with him on the trip an unusual display of Western art—nearly five hundred dollars worth of hand-wrought spurs and bridle bits, the work of his own hands.

The spurs are most elaborate with inlaid designs of platinum, solid gold and silver with decorative engravings that range in price from fifteen dollars to sums rivaling those paid for fine jewelry. Some are made with the "girl-leg" shanks so popular among even the best of cowboys, and are equipped with the improved hinge buttons which do not irritate the riders ankle.

The bridle bits are equally attractive and of many patterns. Some have bars with low gags. Some have high gags and rollers. Another type is of the cruel jaw-breaking kind called the "Mexican ring bit" which he says he is not overly anxious to make, even though so ordered, as only a very slight jerk can break the lower jaw of the horse wearing it. These are used only when a horse is particularly vicious. Causey also refuses to lock the rowels of spurs out of consideration for the horse. . . .

As with every true artist, individuality is the keynote of his creations. The patterns are all different, the steel is tempered with the utmost care, and the long Mexican rowels of the spurs he shows have a ring that is music to any ear and makes us all want to be cowboys.[16]

When Bob Causey's health began to fail he let his general blacksmithing go but continued to make his bits and spurs. He died of a kidney infection in Safford on February 8, 1937, shortly before his sixty-ninth birthday.[17]

Robert Lincoln Causey was an artist in many senses of the word. The few spurs and bits that remain in his family reflect his workmanship—the steel neatly dressed, some inlaid and some overlaid so smoothly as to appear inlaid; designs incised into the steel rather than engraved into the added decorations. To ranchers and cowboys, the RLC brand was indeed the mark of quality.

Chapter 10

Joe Bianchi and the Victoria Shank

Joe Bianchi of Victoria, Texas, dominated the spur business in the southern part of the state for years. His distinctive style was copied by spur makers and is still prized by collectors. The distinguishing feature of most Bianchi spurs is the shank, often called the bottle opener or Victoria style. There are Mexican spurs with shanks of this nature that date back to the 1800s, so possibly Bianchi came by his style from this much older pattern. There was also a blacksmith, Al Smith, in old Harrisburg, now a part of Houston, who earlier made similar spurs, but Bianchi was responsible for promoting the style in the coastal cow country of Texas.[1]

Joe Bianchi was born in Origgio, Italy, August 5, 1871, the fifth of eight children born to Louis and Maria Zafaroni Bianchi. In 1882 Joe's oldest brother, Vincent, immigrated to Victoria, Texas, to work on the railroad being constructed from Rosenburg to Victoria. His whole family, except for his married sister Marcelina, journeyed to the United States to settle near Vincent. The Bianchis and their other children—Paul, Emelia, Joe, Adelina, Joshua, and Henrietta—boarded a ship in Genoa in 1885, when Joe was fourteen. They arrived in New Orleans on December 1, 1885, and reached Victoria on December 24. The father purchased a farm on the Old River Road, and it remained the family home as long as he was able to work it.[2] Joe operated his first shop at Okmulgee in Indian Territory. While he was in Oklahoma, his craftsmanship earned acclaim, for that was the heyday of the Miller Brothers' famous 101 Ranch Wild West Show, and Col. Zack Miller sported a pair of Bianchi spurs with gold inlay. Bianchi later said he beamed with pride as these spurs gleamed from Miller's boot heels the day he led the mile-long parade down the main street of Ponca City.[3]

While Joe Bianchi was in Oklahoma, his brother Paul was blacksmithing in C. R. Alden's shop in Victoria. In May, 1887, a carriage maker named C. I. Howe became Alden's partner in his shop at Juan Linn and Bridge streets. John S. Meyer later bought their shop.[4] Paul wrote to Joe, encouraging him to come back to South Texas. He gave such glowing reports of Refugio County and of the work awaiting a good blacksmith that Joe loaded his forge and anvil and tools, closed his shop in Okmulgee, and moved lock, stock, and bellows to Victoria. The brothers purchased the Meyer property on Bridge Street in April, 1901, and opened Bianchi Brothers Blacksmith Shop for business.[5]

Joe married Mathilde Urban in Victoria on February 22, 1905, but Paul never married. On February 8, 1909, Joe opened his own shop beside his residence at

Joe Bianchi at his anvil in 1949. *Courtesy* Cattleman.

407 South William. Joe was interested in making spurs and bits and Paul in general blacksmith work, so they dissolved their partnership at that time. After that, Paul had several blacksmiths who worked with him: John L. Beck in 1908, J. Frank McCoy in 1913, and Joseph Conti in 1915. Conti served as an army blacksmith in World War I. When Paul died in 1919, Joe was named executor of his estate. Conti had just returned from Europe, and he purchased Paul's tools and shop on Bridge Street.[6]

The ring of Joe Bianchi's anvil was heard on William Street for almost forty years. His shop and nearby home were a meeting place for cowmen and cowboys. The

Stamped BIANCHI inside heel band. A typical Bianchi design, pictured in his Catalog "C" (1925) and Catalog "E" (1932). Could be ordered as shown or plain, with silver shank, or full silver mounted. Silver at base of shank and along top of shank was typical Bianchi mounting. *Huff Collection.*

late Tom Reagan, a spur collector from Beeville, Texas, said, "All the prominent ranchers in this area had Bianchi spurs. It was hard to tell the owner of a ranch from his cowboys unless you knew he was the one wearing the Bianchi spurs. I know a dozen retired ranchers here in Beeville, and they still have their Bianchi spurs."

For years, Reagan borrowed spurs from the older cattlemen for displays at the bank or library during the annual rodeo in Beeville. "Mrs. Dobie would loan me J. Frank Dobie's spurs, and Billy Jones would loan me his dad's, Dick Jones's, which we believed to be Bianchis. They were not marked. They had a straight shank and unusual rowels."[7]

Joe Bianchi made hundreds of branding irons and hand forged hundreds of spurs for ranchers such as Claude McCan, the Welders, the O'Conners, Ed Pickering, and other well-known South Texas cattlemen. After he hammered out a man's brand he often stamped it red-hot onto his shop doors. He could point out Henry Koontz's Texas Star, Tom O'Conner's Buggy Pole, and many others he had made. "I started burnin' those brands because one of my first customers wondered how his would look," he said. "I couldn't see any harm in decoratin' my doors with pictures that cattle and horses carried, so I just demonstrated brandin' right here in my shop."[8]

Uncle Joe, as he was fondly called in later life, entered into all blacksmithing phases of the cattle business, but he was quick to name spur making as his favorite. He put out small catalogs for a number of years. In an advertisement in the January, 1926, issue of the *Cattleman* magazine, he invited customers to write for a catalog. One three-by-five-inch blue-covered booklet marked Catalog E and mailed to Texas Ranger C. E. Miller in the 1920s in a personalized envelope with a spur pictured on it, shows four spur styles and four bit styles. All Bianchi catalogs followed this same format: the same size and color, with four spur styles and four bit styles.[9]

The spurs in Catalog E ranged in price, depending on the mounting, from four dollars to ten dollars, each style available plain or with various mountings, and all with the heel bands turned up for stationary buttons. Each style pictured had a silver Mexican coin on each button and on both sides of the rowel box. Three of the

Stainless steel Bianchi spurs with domed Mexican-coin buttons stamped 1947. *Reagan Collection.*

styles had the Victoria shank and one was a straight shank. All were pictured with twelve-point rowels. The style called Spur no. 1 was advertised as being available in light, medium, heavy, and extra heavy weight as well as in ladies' size. The Victoria shank styles that were most generally seen were not heavy spurs. They had a short section of shank that protruded from the heel band ½ inch or so. On it sat the hook-shaped shank that flattened on the sides and widened for the rowel box. Running down the top of the shank in each style was a silver strip. Heel bands came in widths of ⅝ to ¾ inch, and shanks were 2½ to 3 inches long. On each of the bits pictured, a Mexican coin ornamented the cheek piece where the mouth piece connected, and on one style, three coins that became progressively smaller were placed down the cheek pieces to the rein rings. One style of spurs had the coins placed around the heel bands.

In the booklets marked C, G, and E, Bianchi stated that his goods were mounted with plain silver and Mexican money, but initials or brands or names would be placed on spurs and bits without extra charge. The brands and initials were cut into the outside buttons. Bianchi spurs had no other engravings. All other silver decoration was left plain. The spurs were usually full mounted or had only coins on the buttons or over the rowel pins. One Bianchi spur found on Rocky Reagan's ranch in McMullen County in South Texas was absolutely plain. The same four styles of spurs were pictured in each of the three catalogs. The Bianchi spurs are stamped either BIANCHI on one spur and VICTORIA TEX on the other or HAND FORGED inside the heel

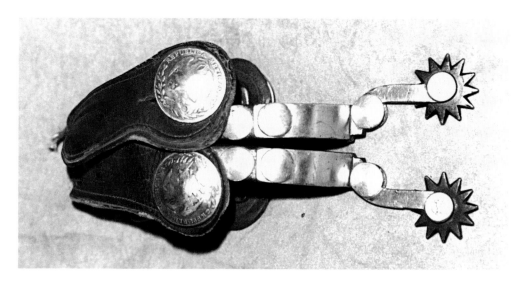

Silver mounted, with Mexican coins on buttons and over rowel pins. Silver dots and plates on heel bands and dots at base of shanks. A variation of "Spur No. 3" in Bianchi Catalogs "C" and "E." *Huber Collection; photo by Dwight Huber.*

bands of both spurs, but their distinctive style is easily recognizable. It appears that the older spurs are the ones marked BIANCHI. It is the theory of some collectors that these spurs were made by Paul Bianchi or when the brothers were partners, and that after Joe opened his William Street shop he marked his spurs HAND FORGED.[10]

Several spur makers, including Buermann and Crockett, copied Bianchi's spurs, but they never matched his mastery of the Victoria shank, although Buermann did a better job of copying Bianchi than most. Buermann's are distinguished by elongated tear-drop–shaped silver mounting on the outside of the heel band and silver mounting on the top of the shanks. P. M. Kelly considered including in his line a spur patterned after the Bianchi style, but he soon realized that Bianchi's distinctive curved shank did not fit into a production line process, and he made only a limited number on special order.[11]

One maker of the Bianchi style was a blacksmith known as Cowboy Traylor. He was a descendant of slaves who had lived on a southeast Texas plantation owned by the prominent Traylor family. It is said that Traylor, the spur maker, had spent time in the state prison, which may be where he learned his blacksmithing; at any rate, he turned out well-finished products in the 1920s.[12]

There are several recent makers of the Victoria style. One is a machinist named Dave Jones of Beeville, Texas, who markets MAD roper spurs. The MAD is a combination of his wife's initials with his. Spurs of the Bianchi type were also made by Koenig of Yorktown, Texas, and Bego of Fannin.[13] All of these men produced hand-made products.

"Bianchi didn't invent that bottle-opener shank," Tom Reagan said. "I have a pair of spurs of that type that belonged to John Cook, a Hereford breeder here at Beeville. These spurs have United States quarters on the buttons dated 1891, 1892, 1893, and 1894, but they are not Bianchi spurs." Reagan told of buying spurs from the widow of Houston-area blacksmith Al Smith. "Smith was making spurs in 1900 or earlier. He made a variety including the bottle-opener style. The majority had thin heel bands, and he often used United States quarters on the buttons. None of the spurs were marked. After Smith had died, my uncle, Rocky Reagan, and I saw his wife. I wanted to buy some spurs. All she had was a little glass display case full of rusty spurs. I bought the whole works for $100, and, disappointed in my acquisition, it was ten years before I got around to cleaning them up. I found three or four pairs of really good spurs, including a pair of gal-leg spurs with the leg in reverse . . . the toe was connected to the heel band. Texas Slim had left a pair of gal-leg spurs decorated with stars and crescents with Smith to be repaired, but he was killed in a fight before he returned for them. In cleaning up these rust-covered spurs, I found a pair of gal-legs with stars and crescents. The majority were small, thin spurs, and two-thirds of them had the bottle-opener shank. It is my opinion that Smith made this style prior to the time that Bianchi made it his trademark."

Joe Bianchi was involved in civic affairs and was an active member of the Victoria Fire Department almost until his death. He and his wife were staunch Catholics and with gifts and money supported the Sisters of the Incarnate Word and Blessed Sacraments and two parochial schools, the Nazareth Academy for girls and St. Joseph School for boys. Joe Bianchi died after a lingering illness on May 29, 1949, at the age of seventy-eight, and his wife survived him by only two and a half years. The couple had no children and left their estate to the Catholic schools they had supported generously during their lifetime.[14] Apparently the Bianchi tools were sold to a small firm in Dayton, Texas, which continued to manufacture the bottle-opener–shank spurs in stainless steel for five or six years. They were marked SADDLEROCK by the button.[15]

Joe Bianchi was a good businessman and a respected citizen. For half a century he sustained the reputation of being a master craftsman in the bit and spur field. Some unknown Mexican blacksmith may have invented the Victoria shank, but Joe Bianchi's products added the term to the nomenclature of U.S. spur collecting.

Chapter 11

The Boones, Blacksmiths since Daniel's Time

Boone has long been an illustrious name in American History. This segment of the spur story deals with the Boones—Bob, Pate, Dee, and their kin, Wallie—all spur makers and descendants of the legendary Daniel. Jerry Clayton Boone, father of Bob, Pate, and Dee, came to Texas from North Carolina. Wallie Boone's father, Duff, was Clayton Boone's half-uncle. After Clayton's father had left home to fight in the Civil War and failed to return, his wife remarried. Clayton disliked his stepfather, and in 1865, when he was twelve years old, he ran away from home. He finally reached Greenvine, Texas, where he stayed for the next several years and worked for another half-uncle, Tom, in his blacksmith shop.[1]

While at Greenvine, Clayton met Joe Campbell and fell in love with Joe's sister, Frances Abigail. She and Clayton were married in Greenvine and lived with her parents, the C. J. Campbells, until after Bob was born in 1883. A daughter, Emmyeann, was next, and a second son, Thomas Payton, called Pate, was born in 1887. When interviewed in 1973, Bob recalled, "Grandpa was postmaster and justice of the peace there in Greenvine. I was six years old when we moved to Baylor County in 1889. We made the 400-mile trip by covered wagon. All that plains country was still open then. My uncle Joe went with us. The ford on the Brazos River about a mile and a half from Grandpa's store was impassable because of high water, and it was 150 miles on north to a town where we crossed the river on the first iron bridge we had ever seen. We went on up the river until we got to Baylor County and a little settlement called Round Timber, twenty miles south of Seymour. My father traded our wagon and team for a store and a blacksmith shop and a little house nearby. He was soon appointed postmaster."[2]

Pate remembered, "Dad made the area ranchers bits and spurs while there in Baylor County. They were just common steel. He didn't mount them, and he didn't mark them. A number of years later when he had a shop in Decatur, he made some spurs that he mounted, but he never did make too many anywhere. He did more general blacksmithing, but all of us boys learned the trade from him." It was here in Baylor County that Bob, the artisan of the sons, first became known for his spurs.

"I was always with my father in his blacksmith shop, mostly getting in the way," Bob laughed, "but that's where I made my first spurs. After I made a few pair, I improved pretty fast for a kid. It wasn't long until cowmen were coming from quite a way to get me to make spurs."

Unmarked spur, identified by O. R. Huff as made by Clayton Boone after he opened a shop in Decatur, Texas, in 1912. Silver mounted gal-leg design with copper pants and shoes. Hump in foot makes more room for rowel pin. Huff acquired these spurs from a man who turned the forge when Boone made them. *Huff Collection; photo by Bob L. Trantham.*

By 1898 the Seymour country was getting too settled to suit Clayton Boone's taste, so he loaded his family into another covered wagon and moved southwest to Clyde, just east of Abilene, where he "set up to do blacksmith work." Young Bob had become quite proficient at making spurs and bits and was by this time mounting them. Pate recalled, "Bob made the first gal-leg spurs that I ever saw while we were at Clyde. In 1900 we moved to Trent, and Papa and Bob had their tools out in the yard where they worked without even a roof over them. Bob made quite a few spurs there, too. He also had a catalog printed stating that he made any style to order, and showing about six styles of spurs and two or three bits. This catalog was mailed out all through the northwest, and it brought him quite a lot of business. Of course, Bob never made a large number of bits and spurs, because he did all hand work, but he made quite a few. In 1901 we moved to Midland, where Papa opened a shop."[3]

"After we moved to Trent in 1900," Bob remarked, "my father saw that I had possibility as a spur maker, and he helped me with the finances. When we moved to Midland in 1901, Dad ran the shop and I made spurs. Dad didn't make any spurs there, but did a lot of general blacksmith work. However, working with him is where I learned the trade. I never worked with any of the other spur makers."[4]

While Clayton had his little shop in Midland, a rancher stopped in to have his wagon wheels worked on. He told them that New Mexico was open country with no fences and no worry and free range with fine grass, and all you had to do to get water was to drill a well. You could fence 160 acres for a horse pasture, but the country had never been sectionalized so you couldn't file on it. In 1901 Clayton sent Bob and Pate out to drill a well and establish a claim on some land twenty miles north of Monument Springs. The boys returned to Midland to get Clayton's horses and learned that their father had sold the place and bought another five miles east of Monument Springs. A settlement called Monument had started four miles east of the springs, and the boys went back and drilled a well there and built a big half-dugout to live in.[5]

"The country soon began to settle up a little bit," Pate recalled. "Jim Cook, an ex-cowboy from the Hat Ranch, put in a general store and post office and established the town of Monument about 1902. Then an ol' boy named Perry Sumerly [*sic*] built a little shack of a blacksmith shop, but he wasn't much of a blacksmith, and he didn't last over a month or two. Dad bought his outfit, and he would drive back and forth from home to operate his blacksmith shop there at Monument."[6]

"Bob made a lot of bits and spurs there and sold them to the cowboys. Bob would make up a bunch, and I'd take them in a flour sack to the roundups and sell them. Dad and I sold several pairs of spurs at the 84 Ranch one time, including a fine pair of three-leg gal-leg spurs which Baldy Williams bought for his brother. His brother was wearing those spurs one day when lightning killed his horse and knocked him unconscious, and it twisted those spurs up. They were sent to a museum in Washington, D.C."[7]

"In Monument is where I made my first pair of spurs, about 1905," Pate continued. "I made a good pair for myself, and Bob put a whole piece of silver on each heel band and engraved in script *TPB* for Thomas Payton Boone. He put silver on the ends of the shanks and on the buttons. After we started our Wild West Show in 1907, I rode broncs with those spurs. In 1920 we were showing north of Dallas, and I hired a German boy as a roughneck around the show. He only stayed a week, and when he left, my spurs left, too."[8]

The Boones stayed at Monument four years. Because his wife's health was bad, Clayton decided to return to Texas and buy the farm at Trent. They left Monument on Pate's seventeenth birthday, October 22, 1904. Bob wanted to go to Montana and cowboy, and Pate wanted to go to Canada, so they told their father they were both leaving. "If you boys will help me back to Trent, I'll give you all the horses you can gather up here," Clayton promised them. He had horses scattered all over the country. Bob and Pate rounded up about twenty-five head that were as wild as deer. They helped the family move back to Trent, trailing their horses along. The grass was good when they drove them into Clayton's new pasture. "We planned to sell our horses to get some traveling money, but they were so wild we couldn't give them away," Pate said. "We decided we were going to have to break them first, and we built a round corral so we could handle them. Word got around that we were riding these horses, and they'd buck like the devil! On Saturdays and Sundays people would come in wagons and horseback and afoot to see us ride these ol' bucking ponies. One day Bob was watching the folks flock in to see us ride those horses, and he said, 'Why don't we start a Wild West show?' The only Wild West shows anywhere in the country at that time were Buffalo Bill's and the 101 Ranch Show. We decided to give it a try."[9]

"All of us Boone boys were in the Wild West show business off and on from 1907, and all of us made spurs at one time or another. I never made many until after I quit the show business, though. Bob quit in 1918, and I kept going until 1922.

"Dad helped us move Bob's show to Weatherford, Texas, and he stayed with us until we showed at Decatur. He liked the town and thought it would be a good place to put in a blacksmith shop. He still did mostly general blacksmith work, and he made some spurs there at Decatur, but he still never put his name on them. Bob marked his BOONE inside the heel band. I never marked mine until the last few years, but I've made more spurs since I've lived here in Christoval, [Texas], than I've ever

Unmarked. Made by Pate Boone in his later years at Christoval. Heavy gal-leg shanks with heel bands cut out in snake design. U.S. quarters mounted on buttons. *Mitchell Collection.*

made. I used to make one-piece spurs, but we didn't have acetylene and arc welders then. I don't make one-piece spurs anymore, and I don't make anything out of stainless.

"When I quit the show in 1922, I gave my bucking horses to my partner. My wife, Inda, and I bought a place south of Fort Worth, and stayed there about two years. For the next five years, we followed the oil field booms, and during the depression we stayed in Houston. In moving around and blacksmithing, I don't recall running into any other blacksmiths who made spurs other than my brothers and Wallie Boone. After I went to Hobbs, New Mexico, from Houston in 1936, where I ranched and had a blacksmith shop, a rancher came in who had a single spur that Bob had made, but he had lost the other one. Bob had done a fine job of the silver on it, and the rancher wanted to know where he could get somebody to make a mate to that spur. I told him that my cousin, Wallie Boone, could. Wallie had his outfit going down at San Angelo then, and he was a good spur maker. I gave him his address, and he sent that spur and had Wallie make a mate to it. Wallie wrote him a nice letter and told him that Bob was the one who made the other spur, and that he was no doubt the best spur maker in the United States."

Bob had taught Wallie to make spurs while the Boones lived at Trent, but he didn't make many for some time. Wallie blacksmithed at the village of Whiteflat in Motley County in the 1930s before he opened his spur factory in San Angelo, where several of his brothers worked for him. The old-timers say there were two boys who worked with him in his Whiteflat shop, and he made bits and spurs on order. He also made farm tools and repaired implements. Tradition has it that he left for San Angelo because of hard times caused by the Depression.[10] Wallie's father, Duff Boone, had operated a blacksmith shop in Christoval near San Angelo in 1900, and then had blacksmithed at Crews for several years before he went to Hobbs, New Mexico, in 1938 to live with his daughter.

Stamped BOONE inside heel bands. "The Kent, Texas Spur No. 3" in *Boone Bit & Spur Company Catalog.* Silver mounted with swinging buttons mounted with silver hearts. Chap guards. Three styles were made: engraved as shown, silver mounted, or gold and silver mounted. Made with 1-inch band, 1½-inch shank, and 1¼-inch rowel. *Mitchell Collection.*

Stamped BOONE inside the heel band of each spur. Wallie Boone made trophy spurs each year for the Texas Cowboy Reunion at Stamford, Texas. Full-mounted with swinging buttons embossed with a star. Straight shanks; eight-point blunt rowels. Oval mounting on each heel band. On inside oval is written TEXAS CENTENNIAL, a star, a Longhorn steer head, and 1836–1936. On outside oval is TEXAS COWBOY REUNION, 1930, STAMFORD, TEXAS. A matching pair given the same year is in the Mitchell Collection. *Wheat Collection.*

Stamped BOONE inside heel band of each spur. Made by Wallie Boone, San Angelo. Steer roping spurs with silver mounting, ¾-inch band, 1¼-inch shank, and 1-inch blunt star rowels. Engraved. *Mitchell Collection.*

"Wallie's start in his spur factory came about due to automobiles," Pate recalled. "When Model-T's first came out, the fenders would droop, and Wallie patented a brace that went across from one fender to another. He had a small factory, and his brothers worked for him. Before long, Ford came out with factory-made braces and that put him out of business. That's when Wallie started making bits and spurs." It is possible that Wallie could have been in San Angelo before he went to Motley County, and then returned. Pate continued, "While Wallie was in San Angelo, he worked several men. He silvered [plated] a lot of spurs and used copper and silver mountings. Wallie stamped BOONE in his spurs with a backwards N. He was one of the first to plate spurs." [11]

The first listing of Wallie Boone in the San Angelo city directory was in 1936. He is shown as the owner of W. R. Boone Company, blacksmiths, at 1014 South Chadbourne, with his residence at 1109 South Chadbourne. His last listing was in 1949, when he and William E. Williams were listed as machinists operating Boone's Bit & Spurs at 1210 South Chadbourne. Wallie's residence was given at the same address.

Boone Bits & Spurs put out a catalog of spurs, bits, "rowls," and horseshoes. Catalog no. 3 with no date shows sixty-three styles of spurs, one priced at $360.00,

Wallie Boone, leaning on car at right, and his crew stand in front of his bit and spur company in San Angelo in late 1930s. *Photo from* W. R. "Wallie" Boone Catalog no. 3.

and thirty-four bits. It also states that the company made stock trailers, horse trailers, branding irons, and D-rings and that Boone specialized in plating pistols. In a statement to his customers, Boone wrote, "I have been making Bits and Spurs for 35 years. For the past six years it has been mostly wholesale business. In the past six years I have made over 20,000 pair." A photo of the W. R. Boone Company at 1210 South Chadbourne pictures Boone, his wife, and fourteen workers. The cover of the catalog pictures "The Largest Steel Spur in the World—16 ft. Long, Weight—400 Pounds." Engraved on it is Boone Bit & Spur.

Wallie came on hard times in November, 1944, when he was sixty-one years old. He had a younger brother, Jack, who had been crippled in an automobile accident. Jack and two other brothers, Bill and Bigham, all worked in the spur factory. Jack and Willie Hawes, who operated a garage adjoining the bit and spur factory, had a dispute over a bet at a marble machine at a nearby cafe, and a fight ensued with Jack on the losing end. Wallie retrieved his brother and took him to the shop to wash him up. Wallie then returned to the cafe to get his wife, Ethel, and his stepson, Edward. He later told the district attorney that he carried a pistol in his car because he often carried cash when he closed his business at the end of the day. When he left the car to go back into the cafe to get Ethel, Wallie stuck his pistol in the waistband of his pants. He said that as he went around the building toward the door, someone grabbed him by the neck and said, "I'll kill you!"

In the struggle that followed, he was hit on the head and back and went down to his knees. Hawes died of a shot in the chest. "My mind went blank, and I do not know if I shot him or not," Wallie admitted. He told the owner of the cafe to send for the sheriff, and he waited for the officer. He cooperated freely with the district attorney, but when his case came to trial he was given a five-year penitentiary sentence for the slaying.[12] In November, 1945, the Court of Criminal Appeals ordered Wallie's case remanded for a new trial, but this second chance did no good. Wallie Boone was convicted and sentenced to jail. Tom Reagan saw Wallie after he had returned to San Angelo about 1952 and ordered a pair of spurs from him. Dr. Reagan recalled, "Wallie Boone was just puttering around his shop. He was a broken man after that trouble. I paid him in advance, and after a time he mailed me the spurs. That was the last I knew of Wallie Boone."[13]

Pate said that Wallie soon went to live with his sister in Andrews, Texas. "I stopped several times to see them. He was in bad health and wasn't making spurs anymore, but he was doing leather work. His sister took care of him as long as she could, and finally had to put him in a rest home in Sweetwater. He died in the hospital in Big Spring on July 11, 1958."[14]

Lloyd Mitchell remembered that "Wallie would often make up a bunch of spurs and run a cord through them to hang over his shoulder. He'd get on a train and ride until he ran out of spurs to sell. Then he'd go back home, and make up a bunch more and go back out and peddle them."

P. M. Kelly also recalled Wallie. "I was acquainted with several other spur makers. Wallie Boone was the only one of the Boones that I knew. That was the workingest guy I ever did see. He would sell everything at a big discount. I was talking with Foster Long in Llano once, and he said, 'Wallie came through here a while back and had a bunch of spurs in a gunnysack, and he just tipped up the gunnysack and spilled them out in the floor and asked what I would give for the pile. I made him an offer, and he took me up!'

"He would undersell us all. Oscar Crockett told me, 'That Wallie Boone beats any fellow I ever saw! He put us both to plating spurs, and the plating comes off and the boys will write in and say, I don't want any of the silver stuff like Boone puts on them!'"

P. M. Kelly kept up with his competitors, and as he remembered events, "TexTan got all keyed up to tackle a number of things, spurs and belt buckles and such, and I heard that they took over Wallie Boone's place in San Angelo after he died. They didn't run that but a little while until they shut it down."[15] Tom Reagan said, "Jack Fuqua of Amarillo was the fellow who bought out Wallie Boone." He had an undated Wallie Boone catalog, no. 3, that had Boone's name blacked out and Fuqua's name and Amarillo, Texas, stamped on it in several places.

Pate moved to Christoval, Texas, in 1954. After his second wife died he operated an antique store and a blacksmith shop with Orville Cohn, his stepson. They made spurs and chuck wagons. Thomas Payton Boone died on September 25, 1980.[16]

The third son in the family, Dee Boone of Henryetta, Oklahoma, said of the spur business, "We all have made bits and spurs, but Bob was the artist. Our younger brother, Clyde, was a pretty good blacksmith himself, but he didn't take to it much. I made my first spurs in Trent after the family moved back there from New Mexico in 1904. The blacksmith trade was just natural with my dad; he didn't know anything else but that. He made branding irons, worked on wagons and did horseshoeing, too. There wasn't much money in making spurs at that time. When we'd move, Papa would throw his outfit up under a shed somewhere and work. He just had an anvil and

Pate Boone's final years were spent in Christoval, Texas, where he had an antique store and made wagons and spurs. He is pictured here in 1975.

forge and one of those old drills you put up on a wall. He had learned to do it the hard way, but if anybody needed anything fixed, he could sure fix it." [17]

"Bob made spurs there at the ranch at Monument before he and Papa put in the shop in town. Bob had a vise, but he didn't have any anvil. He had an old wheel off of a binder, and he dug a hole in the ground and set the wheel in the hole and let it stick up a little. He used that for an anvil, and he made spurs right there. Pate would often take a tow-sack of spurs and tie them onto his saddle and make the round-ups. He'd trade them or sell them for whatever he could get for them. That was cow country, and everybody used spurs.

"We moved to Decatur in 1912, and I left in 1915 to go with Pate and Bob's Wild West Show. Papa's shop was on the northwest corner of the square, right across the street from a livery stable. The shop was just a sheet-iron job like all blacksmith shops, and it burned after I left. Our mother died there in Decatur. Papa died in 1947 . . . in Hobbs, New Mexico.

"Papa made more spurs while in Decatur than he ever had. He'd make any kind that a customer wanted. Of course, in those days, there wasn't any welding. It

Dee Boone, Henryetta, Oklahoma, holding a pair of his spurs. *Photo by Gene Krause.*

was all fire and anvil work, and a man wasn't fast enough to get too many extra made. When we'd get the chance, we would make up two or three pair ahead. It would take about a day and a half to make a pair of spurs. We'd get $7.50 for them. That was a good price then. The first time I ever knew anything about McChesney's spurs and bits, he got $7.50 for the spurs and $7.50 for the bits. Times have changed."[18]

After Clayton's shop in Decatur burned, he rebuilt it and worked a while longer before going to Oklahoma to work in a shop in Poteau. After Dee left the Wild West Show, he worked in a shop across the street from his father. They were just working for wages, eighteen dollars a week, and they had more horses than they could shoe plus wagon work, so they weren't making any spurs. On February 10, 1918, the Boones moved to Pittsburg, Oklahoma, a little mining camp where the mines were running at full blast.[19] Dee had a shop at his house, and he made quite a few spurs at Pittsburg and broke some horses on the side. His customers would tell him what they wanted in the way of bits and spurs, and he'd make them to order. Some liked a long shanked bit and some of them liked a short shank, and some of them liked straight-shanked spurs.

Unmarked steel spurs made by Dee Boone when he was a young man. Large six-spoke rowels and instep chains. *Huff Collection; photo by Bob L. Trantham.*

"We always kept the spurs that we had made that the boys in the Wild West Show had used," Dee said. "I still have one pair of long-shanked spurs that we used. People nowadays use short shanks. The styles have changed during the time that we have been making them. I sometimes put the little tie-down buttons on my spurs. Any bronc rider needs some kind of a tie-down, unless he uses awfully heavy spurs. I stamped a few of the spurs I made at Trent, but I stamp all I have made here at Henryetta with BOONE, using individual letters.

"Bob was in Gordon, Kansas, dressing tools for an oil company when the mine shop in Pittsburg where I worked needed a man, so Bob was hired. The mine

Stamped BOONE by button. Made by Dee Boone, Henryetta, Oklahoma. Steel spurs with high goose-neck shanks. Silver mounted; nine-point rowels. *Mitchell Collection.*

didn't hold out, but we worked at the shop until it closed down. Next Bob ranched out near Ramon, New Mexico, and then his family went to Albuquerque for awhile before they moved to California. Bob made a lot of spurs while in Albuquerque. He was the best spur maker of the lot of us. He was a wonderful engraver, and he inlaid a lot of them. I never did any inlaying at all. All mine were overlaid, which is a lot easier done. While Bob was in New Mexico, Pate and I had a shop in Kilgore, Texas. That was during the oil boom days, and it didn't take long until I was ready to leave the mud and long hours and go home to Henryetta, Oklahoma.

"Spur making is a trade kind of like horseshoeing. Not everybody can shoe a horse. They can nail them on, but they still are not shod. I think to be a good spur maker, it sure helps a man if he has used them. The biggest trouble that I've seen with the general run of spur makers is they can't make them to fit a boot. Oscar Crockett knew how to make spurs to fit a boot. At one time Crockett wanted Bob to come to work for him, but Bob only worked for himself in the spur business." [20]

In 1912 Bob had married Mary Jane Green, whose family lived on Sweetwater Creek. He made her a pair of spurs in Trent before they were married. Mary wore those little spurs in their Wild West Show and in parades. [21] Bob had met Mary in Trent when her brother, Rapp, rode one of the Boones' bucking horses. Rapp wanted to go with the show, but he was only fourteen and the boys were afraid to hire him until they talked to his mother. She said to let him go because she couldn't handle him at home any more. He went with the show and when he had an accident, Bob sent a letter to Rapp's mother. Mrs. Green was a widow with nine children and didn't have much spare time, so Mary, the only girl in the family, started corresponding with Bob. He finally wrote and asked her to marry him. He built a covered wagon for their home and went back to Trent for his bride. She was twenty-one and he was thirty. When they changed from the horse and wagon show to the railroad, they lived in a fancy railroad car. The railroad would sidetrack them at a town and then pick them up after the show closed. They had three or four cars for stock and equipment.

"Our Wild West Show broke up in 1918 because of the war and the flu epidemic," Bob recalled. "Pate's first wife died with the flu, and they quarantined the show and closed us down. By this time, Mary and I had a child ready to start to school, so we stayed in Gordon, Kansas. That's where our last three children were born. I worked in the tool shop there at the coal mines near Gordon. Pate went on with his show for a few more years."

While Bob was working in the tool factory, he didn't make any spurs, but he started making spurs and bridle bits again in 1931 when he homesteaded 640 acres near Ramon, New Mexico, seventy-five miles north of Roswell. The Boones had to haul water twenty-six miles for their stock, and they grew and canned all of their own food. Mary and the girls took care of the garden and the milk cows. Bob and his sons worked for local ranchers doing windmill and blacksmith-type work. They stayed on the homestead for twelve years. [22]

"Most of my spurs were made before and after I had the Wild West Show," Bob recalled. "I never had any stamps and dies. All my spurs were made completely by hand. That's why I never made any two alike. Everything was from raw metal, and the engraving was done by hand with a little chisel and hammer. I had different designs, and I often got ideas out of magazines. I'd put rattlesnakes and road runners

Bronco Bob and Texas Queen

Mary Jane Green and Bob Boone were married in 1912 in Texas. Prior to their marriage, Bob had made the spurs she has on in the photo, and she wore them during their Wild West Show days. *Courtesy B. Gollaher.*

Unmarked, made by Bob Boone. Half-mounted. Large cut-out button with star in center, silver mounted and engraved. Overlay of silver plate engraved CIMARRON on outside heel band. Shank, in the shape of a flower and half moon, is silver mounted and engraved, as is rowel pin cover. Ornate fourteen-point rowel is beveled and has cut-outs between spokes. *Mitchell Collection.*

and all kinds of things on both my spurs and guns. From 1940 when we went to Albuquerque, I did engraving for people in almost every state. They'd send me spurs and guns to mount and engrave. After I went to Burbank, California, I really did much more gun work than spur work. . . . I put BOONE on all of the later spurs that I made in Burbank and also those made at Albuquerque.[23] While at Albuquerque and Burbank, I made fancy spurs for people and often engraved them . . . 'In memory of . . .' and named famous cattle trails or people. I also made quite a few bits. Every man liked his own type of bit, so I'd make them to order like I did spurs. I kept a book of patterns that they could look at to choose from.

"I made a lot of spurs with what we called spoke rowels. There might be six spokes or there might be five prongs or ten or twelve . . . it was up to the buyer. I made all of my rowels by hand and the spurs were all one piece. A buggy axle was the best steel I could get. I'd use silver from Mexican coins, and if I wanted something fancy, I'd go to a jewelry shop and buy a gold ring and cut it up and use the pieces. I'd sometimes take the little colored sets out of jewelry and use them on a pair of spurs, too.

"I didn't melt the Mexican coins; I just hammered them out. If it was a pretty good sized, heavy spur, I might just put the whole coin on it. But I'd often hammer out the silver and then engrave a design. I used mostly swinging buttons, and I generally put the little buttons on the band for the tie-down straps.

"I made one pair of spurs that had an adjustable shank. You could take an Allen wrench and just loosen a screw and set the shank at any length you wanted. If I were using that spur, I'd just set it natural, but every man had his own ideas on exactly how it should set. I also made a bronc spur with an extension over the shank

Unmarked. Bob Boone made this bronc spur with an adjustable shank and extra strap to buckle around the ankle to secure the spur. *Courtesy B. Gollaher.*

for a strap to lace through and go around your ankle to hold the spur securely in place. A man's really got leverage with that spur. Alonzo Boone, a cousin of mine, was at Spring Creek, Texas, making a few spurs like that. As soon as I saw them, I knew he had something, and I decided to make a pair. It should have been patented, but I never did get it done nor did Alonzo." [24]

Bob Boone's spurs are prized collectors' items and difficult to find. His artistry in steel is as beautiful as his silver work and engraving. The West lost a master craftsman when Bob Boone died in San Diego, California, in October of 1974.

Chapter 12

Made by J. O. Bass

The year 1879, when the Matador Ranch was founded in Motley County, Texas, was the same year that James Oscar Bass was born in Atlanta, Georgia, on March 19, one of seven children of J. D. R. Bass and his wife, Lucinda. When he was eleven, the Bass family moved to Young County, Texas, and a year later, in 1891, they loaded their goods in two wagons, and with three yoke of oxen started northwest to the Panhandle. By the time they reached the Caprock and Motley County, they were footsore and hungry, so they put down their stakes at the settlement of Quitaque.[1]

An indispensable part of any frontier town was the blacksmith shop, and young Bass opened his first shop at Quitaque in 1897, when he was eighteen years old. J. O. Bass, Jr., of Plainview, Texas, says, "I don't know where my father learned blacksmithing. He didn't learn it from his father." Being in the vicinity of the vast Matador Ranch, the farrier soon had orders from the cowboys for bits and spurs, so at Quitaque he made his first spurs as a sideline to his regular blacksmith work. His spurs soon displayed the distinctive Bass style that continued until he laid down his tools for good in 1924.[2]

The profile of those early Bass spurs is rather straight, with a long shank, squared off narrow heelband, and swinging buttons. A sample of these early spurs is in the Huff collection. They are stamped on the top of each shank, No. 103. On one side of the shank is J. O. BASS, and on the other side is stamped QUITAQUE, TEX. Many collectors contend that the number is not a pattern number, as is the case with spurs made by A. R. Bayers of Truscott, Texas, but is the number of that particular pair of spurs. That, however, is a misconception. Dwight Huber of Canyon, Texas, says, "My father grew up with J. O. Bass, Jr., in Tulia, and he remembers being in Bass's shop when he was working in the early 1920s, and he can recall seeing orders that came in, and the same numbers appeared on several pairs of spurs. Bass's numbers were pattern numbers, but he chose them totally at random, so that the tenth style of spurs he made might have been numbered 136, but there could have been twenty pairs of no. 136. He kept a ledger of his various designs which corresponded with his catalogs, and spurs could be ordered by pattern number. However, he would also make up a pair by special order on request of a customer."[3]

The Quitaque spurs in the Huff collection are plain iron with no decoration. They have five-point, hand-filed rowels and swinging buttons. The plain round buttons are bradded through a straight strip of metal that runs through slots cut in

J. O. Bass, Tulia, Texas. *Courtesy Swisher County Museum, Tulia, Texas.*

Early spurs (1897–1905) stamped J. O. BASS—QUITAQUE, TEX on top of shank of right spur, and NO. 103 on side of shank. Plain steel except for small silver plate overlaid on each shank and engraved BERT. Swinging buttons and long shanks with slight upward slant. Hand-filed five-point rowels. *Huff Collection.*

the heel band. Bass's son says, "My father stamped only a few of his early spurs on the shank. Most of them have his name on the band and usually on the right spur."[4]

While Bass had his shop in Quitaque, his business grew so that he hired a helper named Willie Weast. Weast learned the art of spur making from Bass and was to become renowned for his spurs in ranching country around Silverton, Texas, after Bass moved to Tulia in 1905. Weast made spurs only on request at Silverton. His design is different from that of Bass but his engraving is every bit as good. He designed each spur as the customer ordered, and the rather wide bands often had the swinging buttons set at a slant, similar to, but not as pronounced as in the method used later by E. F. Blanchard. He also made the popular gal-leg design. He marked his spurs MADE BY W. N. WEAST SILVERTON TEX. under the button.[5]

While in Quitaque, J. O. Bass married Corrie Edmondson. They were later to have a son, J. O. Bass, Jr., and a daughter, Virginia. In 1905 the young couple moved to Tulia, where Bass opened a shop and hired another blacksmith, Nolan Jones, to work with him.[6] Before long, Bass went into the spur and bit business full time, but he always did a little farming on the side. While in Tulia he usually stamped his spurs on the outside of the inside heel band of only the right spur, but sometimes he marked both spurs. Generally, they were stamped NO.   , MADE BY J. O. BASS TULIA, TEX. Sometimes the left spur had the owner's name, as does a pair in Dwight Huber's collection that is marked MADE FOR LEE WALLER, ALBANY, TEX., and sometimes the date was stamped onto the spurs. The letters were imprinted by individual stamps.

Bass's spurs and bits were all one-piece. A 1912 catalog states, "Bits are forged in one solid piece, has neither brad nor weld in them. They are forged from one solid piece of five-eighth inch steel about 10 inches long, especially designed for cowboy

J. O.

Bass

115

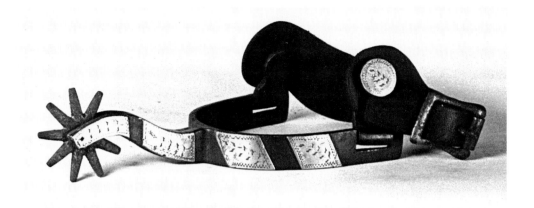

Stamped on heel band MADE BY J. O. BASS, NO. 220, TULIA TEX in small letters. Half-mounted in engraved silver. *Huff Collection; photo by Bob L. Trantham.*

use . . . the top rings are made oblong to protect the leather from buckling, and the bottom rings are so designed to cause the reins to pull to place when tight." On many of his spurs he used a half-silver, half-copper, heart-shaped button on the outside of each spur, but he used other decorations on the buttons, too. The heart-shaped button was, however, a Bass tradition from the early days. He preferred to use buggy axles to forge into his handcrafted works of art, and he paid a premium price for the metal of this origin.[7]

Bass made spurs to order, sweating on silver initials and brands or a mixture of silver and copper decorations, or inlaying them. Each spur was hammered out at the forge and anvil and carefully filed and hand buffed to a smooth finish. No spurs or bits left his shop without passing the close inspection of this master craftsman, and if he was not happy with his work, the spurs were discarded. He developed several innovations, including a curb-flange bit and a lock-rowel spur, which some claim he patented, but his son denies it. "However, once he developed the lock rowel, which was sometime between 1905 and 1910, he made many of his spurs that way," J. O. Bass, Jr., says. In his 1912 catalog, Bass explained his manner of locking the rowels: "The holes in rowels being bored a little large so the end of the spokes will catch in the crotch of shank when applied to horse."[8]

After Bass moved to Tulia, the straps for his swinging buttons took on their special shape, being concave just above the heel band and rounded behind the button. The swinging buttons of this type were generally attached through slots in the heel band, but some swung from hangers attached to the sides of the heel bands. The spur shanks were sometimes decorated with silver arrows, and the heel bands often had copper hearts or silver stars, clubs, spades, or diamonds. He made wide and narrow heel bands, straight shanks and raised shanks, whatever the customer ordered.

L. G. Grubbs of Tulia, who worked for Bass at one time, recalled that Bass was so generous with his time and knowledge that he willingly helped anyone who stopped in his shop and wanted to learn the art of spur making. Often a man would make his own spurs under Bass's direction and at no cost.[9]

In 1914 J. O. Bass won the Metallurgy Award at the Texas State Fair for a pair

Heavy spurs with straight shanks stamped on inside heel band of right spur in four lines, NO. 190(?), MADE BY J. O. BASS, TULIA TEX. Half-mounted with swinging copper and silver heart buttons on outside, silver VM on heel bands, silver arrow through copper heart on shanks. *Mitchell Collection.*

of gal-leg spurs which he fully inlaid and overlaid with gold and silver. This style, which is No. 249, is pictured on the front of Bass's 1912 catalog. They are advertised as having 2½ inch shanks and 1¼ inch twelve-spoke rowels. Full mounted, they have forty-eight pieces of silver, of which twenty are inlaid, plus six pieces of brass mounting. The same spur could be ordered half-mounted or plain. [10]

Bass began issuing catalogs about 1909. They were always small, with only four or five styles each of spurs and bits. Bass marked his bits as he did his spurs, and they were stamped inside the cheek piece. [11]

Bass spurs were sought after by West Texas cowboys and are still hard to come by for collectors. Bass sent out his small catalogs, and apparently he handled all of his sales himself. He kept an order book in which he listed and numbered his orders as he took them. Tom Mix wore Bass spurs, as did many of the Texas Rangers from 1910 on, as long as their work was still on horseback. [12]

A letter from the spur maker to one of his customers, in the collection of the Panhandle-Plains Historical Museum Research Center in Canyon, Texas, indicates the care he took to give buyers what they wanted. The letterhead reads, "Office of J. O. Bass, Maker of Shopmade Bridle Bits and Spurs, Tulia, Texas," and is dated October 15, 1912. It is addressed to Mr. Joe Barton, Jr., Bartonsite, Texas. In part, it reads: "I am quoting you a price of $7.50 on the pair that has the initials on them and $7.00 on the other pair, and I will make the two pair for you for $14.00 and will use special care in getting them out in nice order. I presume you want the old style swinging buttons as that is the indication of your drawings. If you want the staple buttons, they will cost you $1.00 more, 50 cents on each pair. P.S. If you can get me a

J. O. Bass

117

Stamped NO. 364, MADE BY J. O. BASS, TULIA TEX. Engraved silver club and spade along outside heel bands with silver strips on shanks. Silver heart buttons. Nine-point rowels. *Wheat Collection*.

measure of the boots that these are to fit it would help me some in getting them fitted. Take a straight piece of baling wire and bend it around the heel where the band goes and then take a pair of pliers and cut the wire off the exact length that you want the heel band to the end, then lay the wire on paper marking around it both inside and outside with pencil and send me both the wire and the paper with the marks and in this way I can get a perfect fit. I want the paper with the marks to know that the wire didn't get bent in the letter."

The old blacksmith shop was located a couple of blocks north of Tulia's downtown square, but there is nothing left of it today. His tools and a replica of his shop are in the Swisher County Museum in Tulia. J. O. Bass laid down his hammer after making his last pair of spurs in 1924. In a letter from the Tulia Chamber of Commerce to Lloyd Mitchell, the reason given was that the price of wheat had increased and Bass decided farming would be more profitable. However, his son disagrees: "My father's health was bad, so he closed his shop, and we moved northwest of Tulia where he farmed until 1938, when we moved to Plainview."

J. O. Bass spent the last six months of his life in Torbetts Hospital in Marlin, Texas, where he died of cancer on February 3, 1950.[13] He is buried in the Plainview Cemetery near the land that knew the jingle of his spurs.

Chapter 13

Jess Hodge, a Solitary Man

Blacksmith Jess Hodge of Fort McKavett was a solitary man by choice. "There were many in Fort McKavett who would have been his friends given the chance," Louie Lehne said, "but everyone respected his way of life. None of us knew where he came from or anything of his background. There were a lot of rumors. Some said he was hiding out, but that was supposition." He added, "Perhaps Mr. Hodge only wanted to escape something about his own personality. We all respected him too much to ask, and to my knowledge, he never offered the information." Frances Fish, who grew up in Fort McKavett, recalled a visit from her uncle, D. H. Stockton, who had been a cowboy on the Bovina Division of the XIT Ranch in the 1890s. She said he recognized Hodge as a blacksmith he'd known there and he spoke to him, calling him a different name. The blacksmith spoke up quickly, "I go by Hodge here!" [1]

Jess Hodge fired up his forge at Fort McKavett around 1915. "When my family moved to McKavett in 1917," said Frances Fish, "Mr. Hodge was there. No one knew much about him. He stayed to himself and lived alone except for his dog. As youngsters, we'd pass his place on the way to school. We'd often see him cooking his breakfast in an old skillet on his forge. He lived off the land, and he'd cook meat, eggs, and corn all at one time in the skillet and then eat out of it. When he had eaten his fill, he'd set the pan on the ground, and his dog would eat the rest. Mr. Hodge was famous in the area for his gal-leg spurs and his bits that never hurt a horse's mouth. For a man who never advertised, he had plenty of work!" [2]

Facts about Jess Hodge are as elusive as the man himself. Lehne, who lived near the old military post where Hodge had his shop, said, "His name was J. D. Hodge without an *s*." The death certificate gives his name as J. H. Hodges, and the tombstone that marks his grave has J. S. Hodges. It could have been any one of these or none of them.

His real name may have been a mystery, but there is no question about his artistry at the forge. Although he never marked his spurs or bits, their style and quality were easily recognizable to ranchers and cowboys of the mid-Texas area. Hodge's bits and spurs were beautifully designed with a smooth finish and neat silver mounting. The shanks often had beveled edges. He used the silver from dimes and quarters and the copper from pennies for mountings, and on many of his spurs a small silver steer head decorated the top of the heel band with its nose down the top of the shank. [3]

Jess Hodge was born in Alabama on January 18, 1870. Nothing is known of

J. S. Hodge in his shop at Fort McKavett. *Photo from* Menard County History: An Anthology.

Made by J. S. Hodge, Fort McKavett, Texas. Unmarked. Swinging buttons, smooth finish, with plain silver mountings on flat heel bands. Fourteen-point rowels. Silver steer head mounting on top of shanks and down edge of heel bands. Swinging buttons. Some engraving. *Huff Collection.*

Made by J. S. Hodge. Unmarked. Wide heel band has shank set directly onto band instead of on a base as are most of Hodge's beveled shanks. Swinging buttons and tips of shanks are silver mounted. On outside heel bands large silver plates are overlaid and engraved on either end with "JRB" in center. *Baker Collection.*

Made by J. S. Hodge. Unmarked; silver mounted. Large triple gal-leg spurs with shape of the leg mounted on either heel band. Nine-point rowels. Spurs made for Texas rancher Blackie Williamson. *Courtesy Mrs. Lawrence (Blackie) Williamson.*

his life before he moved to Fort McKavett. According to an obituary in the Menard newspaper at the time of his death, he had a son who lived in Oklahoma and two daughters in Alabama, but no one in Fort McKavett recalls knowing of his wife.[4]

"I have pleasant memories of the time I spent around Mr. Hodge's shop as a boy," Louie Lehne said. "There were four or five of us who spent our Saturday afternoons watching him work. Cars came in about that time, but he normally wouldn't work on anything that had to do with a car. If it was a wagon, that was a different story. It wasn't that he couldn't fix a car; he just didn't like to. When I was about eight years old, my little red wagon broke down, and I took it to Mr. Hodge to be repaired. I asked him what it would cost, and he told me the next time my mother baked biscuits, to bring him three or four. He did a lot of work for that kind of pay."

Hodge lived in his shop. The working area was about twenty feet by thirty feet and had a dirt floor. The living quarters in the front were partitioned off and had a wooden floor and a bed but not much else. He cooked on his forge. Bacon and fried potatoes were generally his fare unless a neighbor brought him a mess of fish. Hodge liked to hunt squirrels, and he always had a little stray dog he'd teach to hunt. His friends and neighbors remembered him as a slight man, about five foot six, who weighed only 110 pounds. He generally wore a shirt and pants and a khaki jacket, and shoes rather than boots.

In Hodge's later years he was crippled with arthritis. He quit all of his blacksmith work except making spurs and that became increasingly difficult. He often made both spurs and bits to his own satisfaction, and then sold chances on them. "As I remember, it was a quarter a chance," Lehne said, "and when the pot got up to $8.00 or $10.00, a round piece of cardboard was divided into pie-shaped sections, and each chance-holder's name was put in a section. The disc was then hung in a tree and spun and someone shot at it. The name where the shot hit was the winner of the spurs."[5]

Made by J. S. Hodge. Unmarked. Large spurs with straight shanks, swinging buttons, and chap guards. Mounted. Some of Hodge's larger spurs do not have the smooth finish and fine workmanship seen in most of the smaller ones, which may have been made before he became crippled with arthritis. *Baker Collection.*

Hodge had a friend who worked at the pipeline pump station west of Brady who brought him two bottles of beer every day. When Hodge became too ill to live by himself, his friend put him in the Brady Nursing Home. The people in McKavett collected money to buy him what he needed. Some of his family came to see him, but when he died not long after, none came to the funeral. "There was enough money in the kitty left to pay his funeral expenses," Frances Fish said. "Mr. Hodge was a small man, and once they got all the soot washed out of his pores, he was a handsome man."[6]

Ten or twelve local people attended the simple funeral. The Methodist minister from nearby Mason read "The Village Blacksmith."[7] The inscription on his grave marker at Fort McKavett reads "J. S. Hodges, January 18, 1870 to March 9, 1953." The birth date on his death certificate is January 19, 1869. It seems the only thing certain about the man are the date of his death and his ability to create beautiful spurs and bits.

Chapter 14

E. F. Blanchard, Yucca, Arizona

When he was a young man, Ed Blanchard's occupation was "cinching saddles and pulling bridle reins." His mother, Lilly Ginguely Blanchard, had a ranch in the Magdalena Mountains of New Mexico, and since his older brother had left home and gone off to work, it was Ed's job to take care of the outfit. He also worked for other ranchers, such as the Evanses, who operated two separate ranches, one of their own and another in the partnership of Means and Evans.[1]

"My mother's place was in the Magdalena Mountains south of today's U.S. Highways 266 and 60," Blanchard said. "My mother and her folks had come from Colorado to New Mexico, and they settled east of the town of Magdalena in the Magdalena Mountains, so she had grown up in that area. My father, Herman Blanchard, was reared in Ontario, Canada. He had a brother who lived in Las Vegas, New Mexico, who worked in the mines there, and my father came to Las Vegas and became a miner. I was born in the Magdalena Mountains on September 26, 1894. My dad died of pneumonia when I was fourteen years old, and after that, it was sort of up to me to take care of the outfit. I had an older brother, but he was a miner. He didn't follow the cow business, but Mother kept the ranch in order to make a living. We had a small outfit. We had cattle, but we didn't raise any horses; we just used them. I stayed there until I went into the service in World War II. When I came back from the war, my older brother was taking care of the outfit pretty good, so I left home in 1950 and came out to Arizona and worked as a cowboy up in the Seligman country."

Blanchard said he just headed west and stopped where he could find work. "I had a trailer, my two saddle horses and my spur-making outfit with me, and I set up just west of Ashfork and made spurs there for quite a long time. That was in the early 1950s. I continued working for different outfits up in the Seligman country and making spurs on the side. Like I said, my occupation was cinching saddles and pulling bridle reins. I didn't consider myself in the spur business at that time. The first pair I had made in New Mexico was out of necessity when I needed a pair of spurs for myself. We had a neighbor over around Truth or Consequences, New Mexico, east of where we lived, and I went to his ranch and stayed with him for a while. He was a spur maker by the name of Pankey. He had his shop there at his ranch, and he made cowboy spurs for the boys around the country. I saw how he did it. The ranch where I was working had a pretty good blacksmith shop, so when I got back I just made myself a pair. I got to wearing them, and all the boys liked them. When I'd get an

E. F. Blanchard in his shop in Yucca, Arizona, 1973.

order, I'd go back to headquarters and make up a pair. Finally, I just got my own outfit and started making spurs."

Blanchard's first spurs were nearly the same pattern that he was to continue making, with a wide band and a short shank. In the beginning they were made of plain steel, but in the 1950s, after he bought a ranch forty-five miles east of Yucca, Arizona, he began making them of stainless steel. "I first made plain spurs, but I was soon mounting quite a few of them. I always put a little mounting on the outside buttons, a star or a heart or such, and on request I would put mounting on the outside heel band, too . . . sometimes it would be the man's initials or his brand. I'd put the brand on one side and the initials on the other on each spur."

Blanchard confirmed that he had stamped his name and location in his spurs for a long time, but he didn't recall just what year he began. It was inside the heel band in both spurs. When he made spurs in San Antonio, New Mexico, he stamped them E. F. BLANCHARD SAN ANTONIO NEW MEXICO. He was there a year or so, about

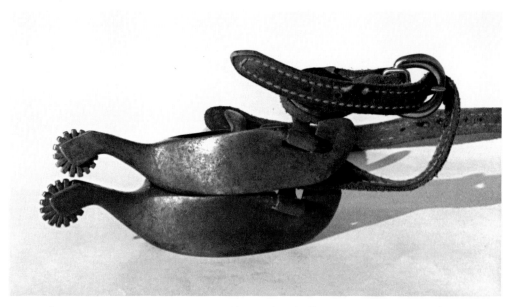

Stamped E. F. BLANCHARD YUCCA ARIZ inside heel band of both spurs. Pictured in brochure, *Blanchard Spurs*, as "No. 2 Goose Neck Spur." 1¼-inch heel band, 2-inch shank, 1¼-inch ten-spoke rowels. Spurs could be ordered in plain steel or stainless steel. Photo is of plain steel spurs, nicely finished with Blanchard slanted swinging buttons. *Baker Collection.*

1948 and 1949, cowboying some and making spurs. When he was in the Seligman area, he continued to stamp them that way. After he bought his ranch near Yucca, he worked some for a few ranchers nearby, such as the Wilsons and the Cooks, but he had just about quit cowboying.

When interviewed in 1973 at his shop near Yucca, Blanchard said, "Spur making soon became a full-time job after I came to Yucca. I now get quite a few orders from stores as well as individuals. The only spurs I make are the styles in my brochure.[2] I've been doing that a long time. I've always had those six different styles. The difference is mainly the shank. My first spurs had chap guards. The first spur that I saw that I liked that had the chap guard was a Kelly Brothers spur.

"I made bits for a long time, but I don't any more. When I got to where I had orders for more spurs than I could make, I just quit making bridle bits. It has been about ten years since I made a pair of bridle bits. They were made to order like a man wanted. He'd generally draw a pattern of what he wanted, and I'd make it. All my work is still handwork from start to finish. I work on two pair at a time. My first spurs were always one-piece spurs. For a long time, I made them out of a Ford axle or a drive shaft. I'd heat the steel and draw it out to the width of the heel band. I had a piece on my vise that held the strip of hot steel up over the anvil, and I'd take a chisel and cut it down the middle and spread it so I could put a loop in it and shape it. One of the biggest changes in my spur making is that I quit that splitting and hammering. After I got an acetylene welding outfit, I decided I could just cut out the shank and weld it onto the band. I welded the plain steel spurs, too. I can't remember just exactly when I began using stainless steel, but it's been a long time. It is a little harder to work

Stamped E. F. BLANCHARD YUCCA ARIZ inside heel band. Another "No. 2 Goose Neck Spur" but mounted with silver bar at base of shank, silver button and a brand on outside heel band. Blanchard's style of slanted swinging buttons. *Mitchell Collection.*

with, and it's a little harder to weld, too. For a long time I sawed the rowels out by hand. Now I have them cut out at a machine shop with a machine that cuts a dozen pairs right quick for seventy-five cents apiece. It's a whole lot cheaper and easier than I can make them. My time is worth more than that."

Just before Ed moved to Yucca from his ranch, his brother Charlie was living in El Paso and was out of work, so he stayed with Ed at the ranch for a while and helped in his shop. After that, Charlie often helped when he was at Blanchard's. Making spurs was Ed's line, though, and Charlie never considered spur making as his profession.

Blanchard remembered his first efforts at spur making. "When I first started, it took four or five days to make a pair of plain spurs. The way I go at it now, I can make a pair in one day, even though I'm using harder material, but I'm set up for doing it. When I first started making them, filing was the only way to get a nice finish on the spurs. Now they can be ground and buffed off. I don't make any with heel bands of less than an inch in width, and generally they have 1¼-inch to 1½-inch heel bands. It's hard to make a real good spur with a narrow heel band that will hold up and set on your boot right. I've put swinging buttons on at an angle ever since I've made them. I've always dropped the slot down at the back, because it gives the button the right angle for the strap.³ I never made any that had turned-up bands with stationary buttons. My spurs set well on a man's boots and have been well accepted, so I have seen no reason to change."

Blanchard mailed out a folder in the 1970s picturing the six styles of spurs he made. Only one had a chap guard. Each could be ordered in plain steel or stainless. The plain steel ranged from $33.00 to $35.00, and the stainless spurs about $4.00 more. Silver brands or initials were $7.00 extra. In the 1950s these same spurs had

E. F.
Blanchard

———

127

Stamped E. F. BLANCHARD YUCCA ARIZ inside heel band of both spurs. Pictured as "No. 4 Drop Shank and Chap Guard" in brochure *Blanchard Spurs,* which shows the six styles made by Blanchard in plain steel or stainless steel. No. 4 is the only spur made with chap guards. Has 1½-inch heel band, 2-inch shank, 1¼-inch ten-spoke rowels. Silver mounting over rowel pins and silver initials, LM, for Lloyd Mitchell, mounted on outside heel bands. *Mitchell Collection.*

brought from $15.00 to $20.50. These spurs were stamped inside the heel bands E. F. BLANCHARD YUCCA ARIZ.[4]

Ed Blanchard never married. He lived on the outskirts of Yucca in a modest white frame house. His shop was in a tin building at the rear of his house. The last half-dozen years of his life were spent in a convalescent home in Kingman, where he died January 17, 1982, at the age of eighty-seven years.[5] His brother, Arthur H. Blanchard, and wife Winifred cared for Ed during this time. The spurs left in his shop when he became ill were sent to Kingman to be sold.[6]

Edward Fred Blanchard never did the volume of business that Crockett or Kelly or McChesney did, but he took the same pride in his workmanship. There was nothing fancy about his spurs, but they were durable and honest. Blanchard spurs are still used in cattle country, riding snug on cowboys' boot heels.

Chapter 15

Adolph Bayers, The Ex–Cotton Picker

Located in an area of West Texas that was once big ranch country, where the way of life was cow work and home was the saddle, Adolph R. Bayers of Truscott may be considered a Johnny-come-lately in the spur business, but his craftsmanship is in great demand.[1]

In an interview in 1972, Bayers said, "I read these stories about bit and spur makers who say they were all cowboys at one time. Well, don't put that down about me. Just say I am an ex-cotton picker!" Bayers's home and shop were located on the place where he was born and reared. "In other words," he quipped dryly, "I've lived here long enough to call it home. I've been here all of my life except for the four years I spent working for Uncle Sam, and he didn't ask me if I wanted the job." Adolph and his wife, Fannie Lois, reared their two daughters at his old home place. Bayers's father was a farmer, and in order to maintain his cultivator and other farm equipment, he always had a blacksmithing outfit, so Adolph learned how to use the hammer and anvil early in life.

"I used to make knives and bits and spurs back in the 1930s before the war. I could sell the knives, but I'd just about have to beg people to buy my spurs and bits. After I came back from the Navy, I didn't have any idea of ever making any more spurs. I turned down lots of orders, but they just kept coming until I finally got back in business. Good advertising was what did it . . . and not the catalog kind! One of the country's top polo players, Harold Berry, is my neighbor. He designed several bits and spurs that I made for him, and being a nine-goaler, other polo players took notice of his equipment and wanted some just like it." Up until the Berry-Bayers innovation, polo spurs had been more on the order of an English spur or a military spur except that they had smooth rowels to meet the requirements of the Humane Society. The Bayers spur on the other hand, had a definite cowboy look to it. In 1959 Wayne Brown had his own idea for his polo spurs and asked Bayers to work up a pair of his design. These also caught on in a hurry. "All the polo players liked them, and I've made more of that style than any other," said the craftsman.

A. R. Bayers made his first pair of spurs about 1930. "They were just a medium-width band with a long shank, which had a slight drop similar to the old-fashioned polo spurs. I wore those spurs around here and finally traded them to William Riley for five bushels of wheat. At the time, wheat sold for twenty-five to thirty-five cents a bushel. Then I traded the wheat for a one-cylinder gasoline engine—one of those that would run a while and pop every so many revolutions. I set

Adolph Bayers in his shop near Truscott, Texas. *Bank Langmore, Photographer.*

that up and rigged it to my grinder and I was in business. I filed that first pair out by hand. You could say they were really handmade!"

From that day on, Bayers's blacksmith shop was housed in a building behind his home, which sits at the end of a sandy West Texas lane northeast of Benjamin. "It takes about a day to make a pair of spurs, depending on how I feel and on how many people go up and down the road. But," he grinned, "That's not a union day! That's from sun-up until after dark."

His first tools were salvaged from the junk yard and rigged by Bayers himself to suit his needs. "I got to thinking one day back in the early 1950s that Enid Justin had everything I needed . . . or at least I thought she should, since she had bought out the McChesney Bit & Spur Company at the time of John McChesney's death in 1928, and Nocona was no longer making McChesney spurs since that part of the business was terminated in 1933.[2] I went to Nocona and talked with Joe Justin about buying the equipment, but then I fooled around and didn't take it. By about 1955, when I decided I could buy it, a junk man already owned it, and I had to buy it from him, but some of it was missing."

The McChesney equipment was in an old building in downtown Nocona. When Bayers bought the machinery there was a laundry in the front of the building where the boot shop had been when the spur shop was in the rear. Some of the machinery was about worn out, but he got things patched up, and he continued using much of it including the dies. If a cowboy's boots sport a pair of distinctive Bayers *espuelas*, they probably jingle with rowels punched out by McChesney dies.

Made by Adolph Bayers for Texas Ranger Charles E. Miller. Unmarked. Full-mounted in silver. Initials CEM on inside heel bands. Bull, flower, and leaf designs and engraved mountings decorate outside heel bands and shanks. All buttons are silver mounted; outside buttons are shaped like flowers. *Courtesy Mrs. C. E. Miller.*

But McChesney machinery had nothing to do with the craftsmanship and the artistic workmanship of A. R. Bayers. Those he developed himself. In his shop were file cards and loose leaf notebooks full of bit and spur designs numbering up to almost 500. The odd numbers were bits and the even numbers were spurs. A sketch of each new style ordered was numbered and put in the book.[3] On the heel band by the button of both the right and left spur he stamped A. R. BAYERS and the design number underneath. Then if one spur was lost, a replacement could be ordered by number. "But to make an exact mate," Bayers said, "I need the other spur. The pattern may be the same, but since they're handmade, each pair is a little different." On each page or card is listed the names of customers who had ordered that particular design. Bayers continued, "If a man wants one design, but with the shank changed a little or the width of the heel band different, I'll make them according to order. They're all hand-done, so it makes no difference."

At the time of the interview in 1972, his plain steel spurs started in price at fifteen dollars, and mounted ones averaged thirty-five dollars. "The main thing that determines the price is the silver work. That takes the longest to do. I cut most of my silver decoration out with a little jewelry saw. I have no dies for this. After the silver decoration is put on, I engrave it with a jeweler's tool. If I cut a design into the steel, I use a chisel and a hammer."

In later years, Bayers made many stainless steel spurs, which were two pieces, the heel band and the shank, welded with an acetylene torch. "Stainless steel is harder to work, because it's so much tougher. I can grind down two pairs of regular steel spurs in the time it takes to grind one pair of stainless. In making steel spurs, they're made in one piece, and an old Ford axle is as good steel as you can get. It depends on the style, but I usually allow thirty inches of steel for a pair. I allow some extra to cut

Adolph
Bayers

———

131

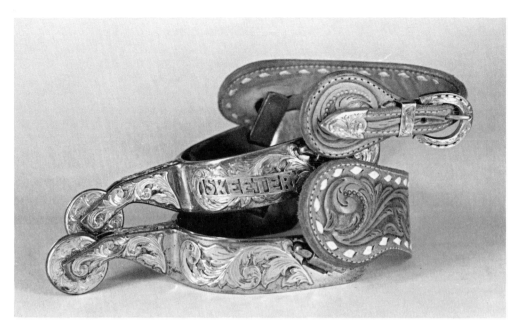

Stamped BAYERS and 526 under inside swinging buttons of both spurs. Stainless steel with full mounting of gold. Smooth rowels are also gold mounted. The name SKEETER is worked into the leaf-design mounting. Gold buckles are on spur straps. *Winston S. (Skeeter) Dennis Collection.*

off rather than come out too short. On the one-piece spurs, I split the steel and flatten the heel bands while they're red hot. Then I hammer the heel band to shape it to fit a boot heel.

"In working with stainless, you can't cut it with a cutting torch. You have to use a hacksaw and a chisel. Then you have to weld the shank on, but it makes a strong weld and buffs down smooth so that it looks like it's all one piece, and it's just as strong. That's true in bits, also. I used to make only one-piece bits, but I weld the mouthpiece onto the cheek pieces now."

After the heel band and shank are shaped, the piece is smoothed off on the grinder. "I can hammer all day, but that grinding wears me down," commented Bayers. With the McChesney equipment and what Bayers had made himself, he was set up to do much of his job mechanically, like shaping the slots for sloping buttons and stamping out rowels, but his spur making was basically handwork.

The buttons were the last step, after the silver was sweated on, engraved, and buffed. Bayers said, "I put the mounting on with silver solder. If you use ordinary solder, the silver will peel off. It has to be red-hot before it flows on there. After being put on like that, the silver might wear off, but it won't peel." His engraving was all done free-hand. To engrave on the steel, he used a diamond-point chisel. Bayers put the buttons on according to the customer's order, swinging, turned up, slanted, or stuck right on the side. As he said, each pair of spurs was custom-made, so their design mattered little.

Made by Adolph Bayers, Truscott, Texas. Full-mounted. The emblem of Texas and Southwestern Cattle Raisers Association is on outside heel band of each spur. Mounted in silver on inside band is DON KING, T.S.C.R.A., 1962. Stamped BAYERS and spur number. *Courtesy Don C. King, secretary-general manager, Texas and Southwestern Cattle Raisers Association.*

For a dozen years the ex-cotton picker made the spurs for the Old Settlers Reunion at Roaring Springs, Texas, until it was discontinued.

Bayers did exquisite inlay work and engraving on guns and also made cinch buckles and D-rings, as well as fine belt buckles and knives.[4] "I won the war making knives while I was on the S. S. Kittyhawk," he quipped. "Those sailors thought a knife would come in handy if they got stranded on one of those Pacific islands. Knives were pretty hard to come by, and I sold as many as I could make."

Adolph Bayers had cancer and died in 1978, at the age of sixty-nine years. Bayers's papers and much of his equipment, including some that had been Mc-Chesney's are in the Panhandle-Plains Museum at Canyon, Texas. This collection includes index cards containing customer information and drawings of items ordered, as well as patterns drawn on notebook paper and cardboard and some customer correspondence. At the time of Bayers's death, he had orders, with checks attached, for fifty or more pairs of spurs. He wouldn't cash a check until he delivered the finished product.

Adolph Bayers's craftsmanship still jingles in time to the easy gait of many a cow pony. Bayers spurs are found on the boot heels of Texas Rangers and cattle inspectors. They are found from Texas to California to England, wherever there is cow country or polo field or horse show arena.

Appendix: List of Spur Makers

The following cowboy spur makers were identified from a list compiled by Lloyd Mitchell of Gatesville, Texas, based on his collection of more than seven thousand single spurs and pairs, and from the collections of the O. R. Huff Estate, Fort Worth, Texas; Bob Taylor, Santa Fe, New Mexico; Dwight Huber, Canyon, Texas; Jack Baker, Sonora, Texas; James Wheat, Mentone, Texas; Winston S. (Skeeter) Dennis, Aledo, Texas; the 1989 Bit and Spur Exhibition at the Nita Stewart Haley Memorial Library and J. Evetts Haley History Center, Midland, Texas; the late H. C. Lewis, Lubbock, Texas; the Pandhandle-Plains Historical Museum, Canyon, Texas; and the National Cowboy Hall of Fame and Western Heritage Center, Oklahoma City. This is presented not as a complete list, but as a start. When a particular spur is described, it is an example and does not mean that is the only style made by that maker. In some cases, only a maker's name or mark is listed. There are many other fine spur collections that were not included in the research for this book. All their owners could add to the following list.

Aarios.
> Name stamped by button.

Adamson, Bill. Kersey, Colorado.
> Stamped ADAMSON under button on heel band. Full mounted. Silver on heel bands. Silver and copper on the shanks. Contemporary.

Allen, Sam. Whitewright, Texas.
> Made full-mounted gal-leg spurs with large rounded legs similar to the McChesney style, with McChesney-type mounting. All-copper stocking and no garter. Prior to 1910. Allen made the spurs and put the mounting on except for the slippers, and his wife mounted those.

Anderson, Ray. Levelland and Weatherford, Texas.
> Maker of fine steel spurs of gal-leg and other traditional designs with copper and silver overlay. Anderson grew up on a farm with cattle and horses. He was farming near Levelland before moving to Weatherford area and had made 200–300 pair in West Texas. Keeps each hundredth pair. Stamped R. ANDERSON and production number by button.

Anderson, T. W. "Andy." Fort Worth, Texas.
>Grew up in West Texas on Matador Ranch. Spurs in Mitchell collection are second pair of five pair cast by L&P Foundry, Pat M. Castleberry, Agnes, Texas, in 1973. Gal-leg spurs full mounted in copper with brass garters and heavy gal-leg shanks are distinctive. Unmarked. (Wheat) Triple gal-leg spurs with this type of leg stamped inside both heel bands T. W. ANDERSON.

Andrews, David. Joshua and Clifton, Texas.
>Began making bits and spurs in 1969. Part-time while working as a saddle maker from 1973 to 1975. Became full-time bit and spur maker in 1975. Early spurs stamped ANDREWS, JOSHUA, TEX and ANDREWS CLIFTON, TEX on inside heel band under swinging button. Later spurs stamped on inside of band with style number, date, and maker's name. Tool steel with brass or German silver mountings. Contemporary.

Ayers, ————. Big Bend.
>Small spurs, stamped under button, AYERS.

Bagwell, Tom. Claude, Texas.
>Unmarked spurs made in 1911 from a tooth from a threshing machine cylinder. Straight shank and heel band. Serrated rowels.

Baldwin, Jos. & Co. Newark, New Jersey.
>(From Holbrook's *Newark City Directory* for year ending Apr. 1, 1871). Saddlery hardware including bits and spurs. "Particular attention given to Orders for the California, Mexican, South American, and Cuban Markets." (Emerson Papers)

Bass, J. O. Quitaque, Texas, 1897–1905; Tulia, Texas, 1905–25.
>*See* Bass chapter. Stamped on right spur only. While in Quitaque, Bass stamped No. ———— MADE BY J. O. BASS QUITAQUE TEX on heel band or shank. Sometimes stamped the owner's name or initials.

Baum, Al. Wickenburg, Arizona.
>Steel spurs stamped BAUM WICKENBURG ARIZ inside heel band of both spurs. ca. 1950. Resemble Blanchard spurs. Opened shop with Chuck Bell in 1959. Started spur maker Ed Costel.

Bayers, Adolph. Truscott, Texas.
>*See* Bayers chapter. Both spurs stamped A. R. BAYERS and the design number underneath. Even numbers were spur designs. Odd numbers were bit designs.

Bego, ————. Fannin, Texas.
>*See* Bianchi chapter. Made Bianchi-style spurs in 1940s.

Belknap Hardware & Manufacturing Company. Louisville, Kentucky.
>Established 1840. The 1940 catalog pictures several spurs of O.K. and short shank styles. They are called "Blue Grass" and stamped on side of heel band. Shapleigh Hardware Company started in 1843 in Saint Louis for Diamond Edge products and was a manufacturer and jobber. Their 1929 catalog lists

iron spurs stamped BLUE inside a diamond (Blue Diamond) on the heel band. Spurs listed in Belknap catalogs of 1930s known as Belknap Blue Diamond spurs. Stamped on outside of heel band by button.

Bell, Chuck. Sheridan, Wyoming.
Quality custom-made spurs for cowboying, roping, and horse training. First spurs made in Sheridan. While working on Flying E Ranch near Wickenburg, Arizona, made spurs for local cowboys. Opened spur shop in 1959 in Wickenburg with Al Baum. Then returned to Sheridan and opened shop at Big Goose Creek near Sheridan. Making spurs there in 1970s.

Bell, Tom. Topsey, Texas.
Made twisted shank spurs, ca. 1910.

Bianchi, Joe. Victoria, Texas.
See Bianchi chapter. Victoria shank. No engraving. Stamped HAND FORGED inside heel band. Some spurs stamped BIANCHI inside heel band could have been made by brother, Paul Bianchi.

Bridwell, L. H. Forestburg, Texas.
Four suits of playing cards engraved in silver overlay. Stamped HAND FORGED BY L. H. BRIDWELL FORESTBURG TEX.

Bischoff, G. A. & Company. Gainesville, Texas.
See Bischoff and Shipley chapter. G. A. BISCHOFF, GAINESVILLE TEX or G.A.B. GAINESVILLE TEX and HAND FORGED stamped inside heel bands both spurs.

Blackwood, Bob. Farmersville and McKinney, Texas.
Maker of blued steel and stainless steel rodeo spurs. Mountings of polished steel. Stamped BB on heel band. Contemporary.

Blanchard, Ed F. San Antonio, New Mexico; Yucca, Arizona.
See Blanchard chapter. Early spurs are hand-forged steel. Later spurs are two-piece welded stainless steel. Decorations are usually only brands or initials. Made only six styles and only swinging buttons, which were set at a slant. It is said he used Arthur Crockett's tools. Stamped E. F. BLANCHARD SAN ANTONIO, N.M. or E. F. BLANCHARD YUCCA, ARIZ inside heel band.

Bohlin, Ed. Cody, Wyoming; Hollywood, California.
Well-known saddle maker. Maker of both cowboy and buckaroo spurs. Stamped BOHLIN inside heel band.

Boone, Bob. Trent and Midland, Texas; Albuquerque, New Mexico; California.
See Boone chapter. Bob Boone was a master craftsman with steel and inlay and also noted for his engraving of pistols.

Boone, Clayton. Decatur, Texas.
See Boone chapter. Father of Bob, Dee, and Pate Boone. General blacksmith. Made spurs while owned shop in Decatur, Texas, 1912–16 or later. No mark.

Boone, Dee. Henryetta, Oklahoma.
> *See* Boone chapter. Learned blacksmith trade from father and older brother, Bob. Made spurs mainly after moving to Henryetta, Oklahoma, in 1925. Stamped BOONE by button or D. BOONE.

Boone, Thomas Payton ("Pate"). Christoval, Texas.
> *See* Boone chapter. Pate made a few spurs in Trent, Texas, in 1905, but made most of his spurs after moving in 1954 to Christoval, where he operated an antique store and made wagons. Heavy, rough spurs. His spurs stamped BOONE or BOONE MKR. in heel band were generally made in Christoval.

Boone, Wallie R. San Angelo, Texas.
> *See* Boone chapter. Cousin of Bob, Pate, and Dee Boone. Learned trade from Bob Boone while Bob lived in Trent, Texas. Owned blacksmith shop in San Angelo during 1930s–1940s. Good quality spurs. Boone often plated his spurs. Stamped BOONE inside heel band. Business was sold to Jack Fuqua of Amarillo, Texas, and operated only a short time.

Bradney, Frank. Canon City, Colorado.
> Prior to 1920. Business card reads Bradney Spurs and Bits. Stamped FB on heel band by button.

Broadway, B. F. Waco, Texas.
> Aluminum spurs, circa 1944. Unusual swinging buttons.

Broadway, L. Waco, Texas.
> Spurs made circa 1944 of aluminum and not marked. Hinged button swingers.

Brown, ———.
> Steel spurs similar to old Crockett's short shank bronc spurs. Stamped BROWN on outside of heel band under button. Plain. No mounting.

Brown, Charlie. Coal Creek, Colorado.
> Contemporary.

Browning, O. B. Pauls Valley, Oklahoma.
> Gal-leg spurs. Said to have been a machinist for John R. McChesney. Stamped OBB twice on heel bands and once on shank.

Brownlee, ———.
> Plain iron spurs. Stamped under swinging button on both spurs, BROWNLEE.

Buermann, August, Manufacturing Company. Newark, New Jersey.
> *See* Buermann chapter. Buermann spurs are always stamped in some manner, most often with a B over-stamped on an A inside a star. Buermann patented his "Star Brand" in 1879. Also stamped PAT'D, BUERMANN'S O.K., HAND FORGED STEEL, STAR STEEL SILVER, HERCULES BRONZE PATENTED, BUERMANN'S PATENT, FORGED STEEL under the button inside the heel band. Arm and hammer symbol (seen in trademarks of both August Buermann and J. R. McChesney) stamped by button on heel band. Thought to be a Buermann

mark on hand-forged spurs. August Buermann Manufacturing Company was sold to North & Judd in 1926, and the Buermann styles that were continued were stamped with a plain star and usually other information such as HERCULES BRONZE.

Butters, Randy. Homer, Michigan.
Stamped BUTTERS. Nice engraving on silver mounting. Contemporary.

Capps, W. M.
Stamped W. M. CAPPS.

Carrol, J. W. Hazel, Oklahoma.
Old spur stamped on side of heel band MADE BY J. W. CARROL HAZEL, OK.

Carter, H. T. San Angelo, Texas
Old steel spur. Silver mounted. Stamped H. T. CARTER on heel band between swinging button and shank.

Cates, Jerry. Amarillo, Texas.
Made spurs part-time beginning 1969, full-time beginning 1980. Stamped OX (1969–80) or CATES and production number (1980 to present) under swinging buttons. Contemporary.

Causey, Robert Lincoln. Odessa, Texas; Eddy and Artesia, New Mexico; Pendleton, Oregon; Rupert, Idaho; Safford, Arizona.
See Causey chapter. Stamped R.L.C. on heel band of spurs and on cheek pieces of bits.

Colorado Bit & Spur Company. Denver, Colorado.

Cox, Bob. Waco, Texas.
A Waco jeweler during 1930s. Ornate drop-shank spurs with cut-out loops on top of heel bands and custom-made eight-point rowels. Unmarked.

Crews, D. E. Pawnee, Oklahoma.
Stamped D. E. CREWS inside heel band.

Crockett, Oscar. Pawhuska, Oklahoma; Kansas City and Lenexa, Kansas; Boulder, Colorado.
See Crockett chapter. Stamped O. CROCKETT inside heel band. Stamped CROCKETT on rim of heel band or inside or outside of heel band.

Cross, Mark. New York, New York.
English-style plated spurs in leather case. Firm founded in 1845. Dealt in leather goods, saddles, harnesses, and trunks. Now deals in luggage, handbags, etc. Stamped inside heel band MARK CROSS CO.

Demar, ——.
Handcrafted stainless steel spurs.

Denver Buckle Company. Denver, Colorado.
Stainless spurs. Stamped DENVER BUCKLE on outside of heel band.

Dewsbury, John, and Son, Ltd. Littleton Street, Walsall, England.
From catalog circa World War I: "Registered Trade Marks. The following Trade Marks are registered against infringement throughout the principal countries of the world." Included are the following, which can be found stamped on bits, stirrups, and spurs: V. S. NICKEL; J. D. & S.; a picture of a kangaroo with KANGAROO under it; a picture of a kangaroo only; DEWRALEX (said to be the best quality of rustless metal); VICOLETTE (same quality of metal as Dewralex but with less perfect finish); and a picture of a hand with HAND BRAND stamped on it. "The above metals are a result of 35 years experience in Special Metals for Bits, Stirrups and Spurs. . . ." (Emerson Papers and collection)

———. Coville, Washington.
Bronze spurs with white metal buttons. Stamped E-M inside heel band.

Eldonian Stainless Steel Riding Hardware. Walsall, England.
Manufactured by George Shelton, Ltd., distributed in the U.S.A. by North & Judd Mfg. Co., New Britain, Connecticut. Post–World War II. Stamped on top edge of heel band of each spur STAINLESS STEEL, ELDONIAN. (Emerson)

Ellick, Greek, 4-E Spur Shop. Dexter, Kansas.
Black steel spurs with small bronze rowels. Stamped under shank with modern-style G. Contemporary.

———.
Small spurs, stamped ERN.

Fleming, ———.
Full-mounted double gal-leg spurs sold by Visalia Stock Saddle Company of California. Stamped VISALIA inside both heel bands. Some spurs stamped on both inside buttons S.F. in center, VISALIA STOCK SADDLE CO. around the edge of buttons. A pair with narrow, tapered heel bands and slightly dropped shank with chap guards. *12*-point rowels and engraved silver inlay. Made by Fleming in early 1920s and sold by Visalia. Stamped. Saddlemaker D. E. Walker was the founder of the company in 1870 in San Francisco. C. D. Magers was assistant manager from 1935 to 1940, then manager. Became partner in a wholesale silver manufacturing company in 1945 and bought out partner in 1955. Purchased Visalia in 1964. Company moved to Castro Valley, and in 1971 to Grass Valley.

Fogg, H. L.
Straight shank spur, stamped H. L. FOGG under button.

Ford, R. F. Kermit and Water Valley, Texas.

Friend, Lee. Christoval, Texas.
Stamped FRIEND and production number on outside of inside heel band. Contemporary.

Garcia, Guadalupe S. Elko, Nevada.

Stamped G. S. GARCIA inside heel band of one spur; ELKO NEV inside heel band of other spur. Also stamped G. S. GARCIA MAKER ELKO NEV and G. S. GARCIA ELKO NEV. with the N backwards, thought to have been used 1910–20. Born in San Luis Obispo, California (some say in Sonora, Mexico, 1864). Apprenticed at Arana Saddle Shop, San Luis Obispo. In partnership in 1882 with a Mr. Brewster in a saddle shop at Santa Margarita, California. Arrived in Elko, Nevada, in November, 1893, and opened a shop (maybe 1896). First illustrated catalog issued in 1903. Garcia had three sons, Walter, 1899–1929; Les, born 1901; and Henry, born 1910. Les and Henry became spur makers.

In 1920, G. S. Garcia opened a second shop in Salinas, California, and turned the Elko business over to his sons in 1932. He died in 1933. Three years later, the Elko shop was moved to Salinas and closed during the war because of material shortage. It reopened in 1946. In 1957, Les sold out to Henry, who continued with the business until 1979, when it was purchased by J. M. Capriola Company and returned to Elko. The new owner was a former Garcia employee.

Garcia, Les. Reno, Nevada.

After Les sold to Henry in 1957, he retired in Reno for a few years before he began making bits and spurs again. Stamped LES GARCIA RENO under button or inside heel band.

Glover, Walter. Amarillo, Texas.

Stainless steel spurs with brass decoration. Circa 1950. No mark.

Goben, G. F. (or G. A.). Johnson City, Texas.

Stamped G. F. (OR A.) GOBEN on shanks.

Grijalva, Eduardo. Magdalena, Sonora, Mexico.

A nice pair of gal-leg spurs marked EG (star) by button. Engraved silver mounting.

Grubbs, L. G. Tulia, Texas.

Grubbs learned spur making from J. O. Bass. Stamped on outside band of right spur and inside of left spur, MADE BY L. G. GRUBBS 6–8–1970.

Hall, Carl D. Comanche and Gustine, Texas.

Spurs with flower design and fancy gal-legs. 1¼-inch heel bands, nickel silver mountings, 2½-inch raised shanks with chap-guards. Stamped HALL under button around edge of heel band on both spurs. Contemporary.

Hartley, ————. Amarillo, Texas.

Stamped OX.

Hartzell, George. San Angelo, Texas.

Pioneer Shop in San Angelo.

Helvey, ————. Abilene, Texas.

Stamped H on button.

Hildreth, Tom L. Sacramento, California.

> Hildreth died about 1906. He stamped his spurs behind the button across the end of the shank HILDRETH and under that SAC.

Hininger, J.

> Small brass spurs.

———.

> Heavy spurs stamped HLH under swinging button.

———.

> Stamped HLT.

Hodge, Jess. Fort McKavett, Texas.

> *See* Hodge chapter. Some spurs identified by silver steer head with nose down top of shank and horns around heel band. Not on all spurs. No mark.

Hollis, Gerald. Beeville, Texas.

> Made of twisted stainless steel rods. No mark. Contemporary.

Holman, Ed. Sheridan, Wyoming.

> Stamped E.H. under button on both spurs. Silver diamond inlaid on top of shanks.

Holmes, T. L. Sacramento, California.

> Older spurs inlaid. Newer spurs overlaid. Gal-leg style has toe pointed like a ballet dancer. Marked TLH over SAC on swinger for instep chains. Some spurs not marked.

Huck, ———.

> English-style spurs. Stamped with HUCK inside an anvil on inside of heel band.

Huff, O. R. Fort Worth, Texas.

> *Learned to make spurs from Laney Kilgore, who did not mark his spurs. Made circa 1935. Unique horsehead shanks overlaid with gold and silver, engraved and set with colored stones on heel bands. Marked with overlaid D+ (D Cross) on both spurs. Huff's gal-leg spurs mounted with silver and copper and finely engraved.*

Johnson, Tom, Jr. Albany, Texas; Pauls Valley, Oklahoma (at McChesney's); Dalhart, Texas (at Kelly Bros.); Dalhart, Texas.

> Johnson learned spur making from his father in Coleman, Texas. P. M. Kelly said, "When Tom moved his shop to Albany, I think his father had died. He went from Albany to work for McChesney, and that's where I met him. When I opened my shop in Dalhart in 1911, he came to work for me. Tom was one of the best and fastest hand-workmen I ever saw. He put a fine finish on his spurs. People would say, 'That's a Tom Johnson job!' When I geared up for production, Tom wanted to stay with the hand work, so he opened his own shop there in Dalhart, which he operated until his death in 1915. Tom had married my sister, Lena, and after his death my company continued to

fill his orders as Tom Johnson spurs until Lena's death in 1917. I wrote to the customers then, explaining that Kelly Brothers had been making the Tom Johnson spurs for the past two years and would continue if they so desired. Tom did not mark his spurs, and the spurs we made in his name had no mark."

Kelly said that Johnson specialized in what Kelly called a "goose-neck" shank, referring to the shape of the raised shank and not the shank's terminating in a goose head. Mitchell and Huff believed that his gal-leg spurs have flat legs and no garters, are half-mounted, and the wriggled engraving is flat on the tops. The mountings most likely seen on Johnson's spurs were also used by McChesney and Kelly, according to Huff.

Johnson, Tom, Sr. Coleman, Texas.
   Blacksmith shop circa 1910 in Coleman. No mark.

Jones, David. Beeville, Texas.
   Bianchi-style spurs made circa 1974. Called MAD roper spurs, from a combination of initials of Jones and wife.

———.
   One-piece molded spur with solid piece that goes under the instep. Stamped K.C.

———.
   Half-mounted spur with brass and silver. Kelly-type. Stamped K&C under button.

Kapish, George. New Mexico.
   Blacksmith on TO Ranch in northern New Mexico. No mark on unmounted spurs.

Kelly, P. M. Childress, Texas, 1903; Hansford, Texas, 1907–10; Pauls Valley, Oklahoma (McChesney), 1910–11; Dalhart, Texas, 1911–25; El Paso, Texas, 1925–35 (Kelly in Mexico 1935–39), 1939–65.
   See Kelly chapter. Kelly spurs are always marked, except those he made in the name of Tom Johnson 1915–17 after Johnson's death. The stamp is usually on the heel band by the button. Kelly spurs are marked KELLY BROS., KB&P, KELLY BROS & PARKER, KBP, KELLY, or RODEO.

Kerry, ———.
   Fancy spurs with coins. Resemble Wallie Boone's spurs. Made circa 1936. Stamped KERRY inside heel bands of both spurs.

Klapper, Billy. Childress and Pampa, Texas.
   Cowboy turned full-time spur maker when he opened his shop in Childress in 1968. Specializes in custom and personalized spurs. Contemporary. Stamped KLAPPER and production number below button on heel band.

Klecka, F. Fort Gates, Texas.
   Stamped F.K., according to Mitchell.

K Manufacturing Company. ———.
Small spurs with buckles or loops at the ends of the heel bands.

Kittleson, John. Loveland, Colorado.
Pamphlet pictures ten styles of blued steel spurs with three silver strips mounted on heel band and swinging buttons set at an angle. A variety of rowels. Only other mountings are initials. Trademark has a kettle with a rising sun.

Koenig, ———. Yorktown, Texas.
Made Bianchi-style spurs.

Kyle Products, Inc. El Paso, Texas.
Had been Kyle-Pettigrew. Plain stainless steel spurs with ⅜- to ¼-inch band, stamped behind slanted swinging buttons.

Lindley, Jerry. Weatherford, Texas.
See Lindley chapter. Stamped LINDLEY, production number and pattern number on both spurs under buttons. Made first spurs in 1970. Learned to make one-piece spurs from Milton McCowen. Full-time since 1984.

Loyd, ———.
Silver- and copper-mounted gal-leg spurs decorated with hearts, clubs, and diamonds and stamped LOYD on inside heel band by button on both spurs.

McChesney, J. R. Broken Arrow, Oklahoma; Gainesville, Texas; Pauls Valley, Oklahoma.
See McChesney chapter. Many of McChesney spurs not marked, yet their distinctive style is easily recognized. Some stamped deep in heel band with large capital letters, MCCHESNEY. After Nocona Boot Company purchased the bit and spur company in 1926, MCCHESNEY was stamped in small letters on the outside of the heel band under the button. Spurs were often plated during the Nocona ownership.

McCowen, Milton. Clarendon, Texas; Hamilton, Montana.
Stamped MCCOWEN in small caps under slanted swinging button with a number on the inside heel band and a different number on the button strap.

Mahan, Larry. El Paso, Texas.
Stamped L.M.

Main & Winchester. San Francisco, California.
Stamped FORGED on outside of heel band by button. Also stamped PAT'D FEB. 6 1877. Leather spur straps are stamped with a medallion reading across the top MAIN & WINCHESTER and across the bottom SAN FRANCISCO, with MAKERS in the middle.

Markel, D. Tucson, Arizona.
Markel died in pickup accident circa 1977. Stamped with ligatured initials (DM) under buttons on spurs and inside cheek piece on bits.

Markel, Dennis. Tucson, Arizona.
> Stamped with ligatured initials (DM) like his father's. Pair has DEAN mounted on sides of heel bands. Contemporary.

Martin, J. Fisher.
> Gal-leg spur made in 1918, according to D. C. Cunningham, San Angelo, Texas.

Martin Zephyr Spurs. Los Angeles, California.
> Martin began making Airplane Metal spurs with the trade name Zephyr prior to 1936 at the start of the aluminum business.

Maxwell, Henry, et al. London, England.
> Steel box spurs. Stamped MAXWELL on wedge that slips into a slot in a small brass or steel box embedded in boot heel. Invented circa 1820.

Merchant, W. Buda, Texas.
> Recent maker of fancy spurs.

Mesh, ———.
> Said to be Navajo bull rider.

Messenger, Loyd. Denton, Texas.
> Flat, heavy gal-leg spurs. Stamped deep inside of heel band on outside, LOYD MESSENGER. Sometimes did only mounting.

Mitchell, B. T.
> Stamped HAND MADE and B. T. MITCHELL.

Mitchell, M. C.
> Shop made spurs with copper decorations and silver initials LWM for Lloyd W. Mitchell.

Montaya, Tony. California.
> Hand-forged spurs with name inscribed inside heel band.

Moore, ———. Abilene, Texas. Moore Spurs (Glynard, Kyle, and Wayland), Matador, Texas.
> Custom spurs, bits, stirrups, and buckles. Fine spurs of the Bayers style with unique silver mountings. Glynard says, "It takes about ninety man hours to make a pair of spurs, sixty hours on the bits, and ten to twenty on the buckles. The spurs are made of one piece of mild steel, bent and tempered. They are made only on order to fit each individual. They are made only for the working cowboy. The designs and brands are made of nickel silver. Our customers prefer the pre-rusted look, as it makes the silver show up."

Morales, M. Portland, Oregon; Los Angeles, California.
> One-piece, inlaid spurs. Advertises in catalog, "Bits, Spurs, & Silver Trimming for the Saddle"—cowboy and buckaroo. Stamped with stylized M under button on outside of heel band or inside heel band or on chain swinger.

Morrison, Roy. Comfort, Texas; Montrose, Colorado.
>Roy Spurs. A 1974 ad shows a spring-tempered stainless steel slip-on spur with brass rowels. In 1983 the company advertised, "Roy is making bits & spurs again. Order now!" ROY stamped on button strap.

Nance, Joseph Johnson. Ozona, Texas.
>Born near Beeville, Texas, March 17, 1870. Opened blacksmith shop in Ozona in late 1890s. He and a partner later opened Nance and Friend Hardware Company. In 1907 the Nance family moved to a ranch near Sheffield. The ranch was sold in 1911, and they moved into Sanderson. J. J. Nance served as sheriff of Terrell County for twelve years. He died in 1947. It is said Nance put silver steer-head mounting on top of spur shank and band, as did Jesse Hodge. He also made bits.

North & Judd Manufacturing Company. Middletown, Connecticut.
>*See* North & Judd chapter. Stamped with anchor on spurs, bits, and hardware since 1879. Stamped a small star and PAT'D on Buermann styles after acquiring that company in 1926. Also stamped HERCULES BRONZE or STAR STEEL SILVER on outside of spur after acquisition.

Overton's Bits & Spurs. Tyler, Texas.
>Made circa 1948.

Overton, Dennis. Seymour, Texas.
>Stamped OVERTON. Maker of cowboy spurs. Contemporary.

————.
>Silver-mounted spurs. Stamped P.G. under button.

Ownby, Danny. Crowell, Texas.
>Stamped OWNBY on heel band. Uses A. R. Bayers's engraving tools. Contemporary.

Palmer, Cowboy. Abilene, Texas, area.
>Heavy spurs with overlay. Made spurs while in prison in Huntsville, Texas. Died in prison circa 1959. One pair mounted in gold brought from New York by sheriff. Unmarked.

Pardue, Steve. Aledo, Texas.

Partrade Company. Tennessee.
>A spur importer.

Peal, ————. California.
>No rowel. Stamped small PEAL'S inside heel band.

Penitentiary Spurs, Texas and Colorado.
>During the 1930s inmates had materials available for crafts and were encouraged to learn a trade. Spurs were often unstamped. Often made of brass or monel (shiny metal used before stainless); mother-of-pearl often used in decoration. Later spurs were engraved. Rowel spokes often resembled little boots. Mitchell acquired last pair in 1974, made by "Pee Wee." Tag on spurs

gave maker's name, serial number, and unit. Marked T.P.S., Texas Prison System. Beautiful spurs were also made by inmate #4307, named Cox, in the Colorado State Prison in Canyon City while serving a murder sentence from 1880s until he died in 1926. He was a craftsman who taught spur making to other inmates.

Petmecky, Joseph Carl. Austin, Texas.

Born in Austria-Hungary on August 12, 1842. At the age of three, with a group under the leadership of Prince Solms, he and his family sailed from Antwerp, Belgium, for Texas and settled in the New Braunfels area. In 1851, Joseph became an apprentice to an Austin gunsmith named Owens. When Owens died, Petmecky, fifteen years old, continued the business under the name J. C. Petmecky. Soon a noted gunsmith, he made rifles for Sam Houston and Texas Rangers Sul Ross, Ben McCullough, and Big Foot Wallace. He was also well known for his spring-tempered steel spurs, which came to be called Pet Makers. Petmecky brought specialists from Sweden for his precision iron work. He made spurs from early trail-driving days through the 1890s. They were prized by ranchers and cowboys alike.

In the Petmecky papers are sketches of two of his spur designs marked 1872 on the buttons and PETMECKY on the shanks. One, known as the spring shank spur is the classic O.K. spur with the curved shank. The second design shows the same four-button style with a straight shank. It was said he sold his patent on this O.K. style for a "mere pittance." The new owner of the Petmecky design was most likely August Buermann, whose name is now linked to the O.K. spur. J. C. Petmecky died August 16, 1929. There is a Mexican-style spur made by Petmecky in the Panhandle-Plains Historical Museum.

Phillips & Gutierrez. Cheyenne, Wyoming.

Raphael Philo Gutierrez was born in 1889 in northern California and by 1905 was making bits and spurs in Sacramento. He worked for several large saddle companies and made many spurs and bits for G. S. Garcia in Elko, Nevada. In 1917, he and Bill Phillips opened their own shop in Cheyenne, Wyoming. Their catalog pictures nineteen styles of spurs and twenty-three bits. Stamped inside heel band PHILLIPS & GUTIERREZ CHEY WYO. Phillips & Gutierrez closed after only one year, and Gutierrez had a new partner named Estrada in 1920 in San Francisco. Juan Estrada learned the art of bit and spur making from Garcia and later worked for M. B. Staunton. In 1940, Gutierrez dissolved the partnership and continued to make spurs in his home until his death in 1958. Stamped R. GUTIERREZ, 1084 LECONTE, SAN FRANCISCO. A true craftsman.

Pliska, John. Midland, Texas.

Blacksmith born in Teene, Czechoslovakia, in 1879. Moved to Flatonia, Texas, in 1897. Pliska worked in Flatonia, Moulton, and Meeks until 1903, when he started to Mexico but took a job in the shop of W. A. "Greasewood" Smith in Midland. He also worked for the C. C. Slaughter Ranch for six months. He and his brother-in-law, John Hundle, built a shop in 1909.

Hundle left the partnership in 1910. Pliska operated shop until death in 1956. He made spurs, bits, branding irons, and rowels and did general blacksmith work. He did not mark his spurs. An airplane built by Pliska in 1912 is on exhibit at the Midland Airport. Pliska rowels were collected by noted author J. Evetts Haley for the Panhandle-Plains Museum, Canyon, Texas.

Powder River. Baker, Oregon; Provo, Utah.
Stamped POWDER RIVER under button on inside turned-up heel band. Silver mounted and engraved. Shown in 1935 Denver Dry Goods catalog as the "Diamond K" spur, Barker, Oregon.

Qualey, Tom. Joseph and Grangeville, Idaho.
Stamped QUALEY BROS. JOSEPH, IDAHO (early 1930s to 1937) or QUALEY. Born 1903 in Idaho. Began bit and spur making in mid-1920s. Partnership with brothers dissolved in 1937. In 1953, worked for Ray Holes Saddlery but continued to make spurs until his death in 1976.

Rawhide. San Diego, California.
Manufacturers, jobbers, and importers, 1970s. RAWHIDE stamped in back of heel band.

Renalde Company: Renalde & Crockett; Renalde, Crockett & Kelly. Denver and Boulder, Colorado.
See Crockett and Kelly chapters. James Renalde was founder and owner of Denver Metals Foundry, makers of buckles and saddle hardware, and of Renalde Company, makers of aluminum spurs and bits begun in 1938. Renalde acquired Crockett Bit & Spur Company in 1951 and P. M. Kelly & Sons in 1965. Catalogs were carried as *Crockett & Kelly Bits Spurs by Renalde*. In 1973, manufacturing was begun in Crockett's Boulder plant and the finish work was done in the Denver factory at Renalde's original location, 1525 18th Street. There were seventy-five employees. The Company was sold in 1979 and was moved to Broomfield, Colorado, as Crockett & Kelly, Inc., but in the mid-1980s, the company was closed. Bits and spurs were stamped CROCKETT, KELLY, RENALDE or CR inside a horseshoe. Stamped on button hinge or on heel band by button.

The Ricardo Metal Manufacturers. Denver, Colorado; Victoria, Texas.
Catalogs in Panhandle-Plains Historical Museum are dated: 1953, Denver, Colorado; 1971, Victoria, Texas; 1977, Denver, Colorado. Mostly cast aluminum spurs but some steel. The 1953 catalog advertised "Sterling Silver overlaid on nickel plated brass . . . polished nickel finish with bronze decorations." Ricardo also had a line with swivel buttons. Spurs stamped in various places in several ways: RICARDO, DON RICARDO in script, or RICARDO and NICKEL SILVER.

Rodeo. El Paso, Texas.
See Kelly chapter. Economy line made by P. M. Kelly & Sons. Stamped RODEO by button.

————. LaPryor, Texas.

Spurs made for H. R. Routt by LaPryor blacksmith circa 1910. Spurs made from Model-T axle. Decorated with Mexican coins over rowel pins. Stamped only H. R. ROUTT, owner's name.

Rowe, W. T., & Sons. Austin, Texas.

Stamped W. T. ROWE AUSTIN TEX or ROWE & SONS. Made spurs with four buttons like straight shank O.K.s. Rowe an Austin saddle maker prior to 1900.

Russell, Howard. Gatesville, Texas.

Blacksmith. Made molded brass spurs circa 1930. Stamped RUSSELL under shank.

Saddlerock. Dayton, Texas.

Spurs with Victoria shank of recent make. Company said to have acquired Bianchi's tools. Stamped SADDLEROCK.

Sasse, Henry. Gatesville, Texas.

Blacksmith and spur maker in 1920s. Made heavy iron spurs.

Scheider, ————. Castel, Texas.

Spurs like small O.K.s. Made before 1900. No mark, according to Mitchell.

Schnitger, ————. Gilette, Wyoming; Hollywood, California.

Stamped SCHNITGER in one spur and GILETTE, WYO. in the other. Worked for Edward H. Bohlin in 1937 in Hollywood.

Schuessler, Adam. Fredericksburg, Texas.

Blacksmith circa 1895.

Sellers, Elmer. Floydada, Texas.

Name stamped on side. Well known for his miniature spurs and bits.

Shelton, Audie. Fort Worth, Texas.

Blacksmith in stockyards area during heyday of horse and mule business. Used brass for buttons.

Shelton, Sam. Fort Worth, Texas.

Nephew of Audie Shelton. Pair of spurs and bits in Huff collection made for father, W. T. Shelton, in 1940.

Shipley, Charles P. Kansas City, Missouri.

See Bischoff and Shipley chapter. Shipley bought the shops of G. A. Bischoff and Oscar Crockett in 1916. Early Shipley spurs are Bischoff and Crockett styles. When Crockett became shop foreman, Bischoff styles were generally discontinued. Shipley sold bit and spur business to Oscar Crockett in January, 1920. Stamped inside heel bands CHAS SHIPLEY K. C. MO.

Shirley, Earlon. Memphis and Tahoka, Texas.

Stamped SHIRLEY in script and production number.

Silver Mark.

Light-weight spurs that slip on heels.

Silver Tip Mfg. Chico, California.

Texas-style spurs of stainless steel, aluminum, stainless nickel, and sterling silver.

Sims, Ed, Spur Company. Uvalde, Texas.

Stainless steel spurs for roping, cutting, and barrel racing. Gal-leg style also made. Brass decorations and letters for initials and names. When roper Ed Sims couldn't get a pair of spurs that would stay down on his heels, he decided to make his own. That led to the spur business, which began in 1947. His spurs are cast and have brass rowels and initials. Sims, a native of Post, Texas, joined the R.C.A. in 1947 and roped calves for the next fifteen years. After opening his spur business in Uvalde, Sims continued competition team roping. Sims spurs have been popular with ropers, barrel racers, and pleasure riders. Stamped SIMS on inside heel band under swinging button.

Smith, Al. Old Harrisburg (Houston), Texas.

Made spurs of the Bianchi style prior to Bianchi, with narrow shanks and heel bands using coins for buttons. No marks.

Star Steel Silver. Wastego, Illinois.

This company patented an O.K.-style spur, No. 763525, in 1908.

Stephenson, Isaac. Darrouzett, Texas.

Pair in Panhandle-Plains Museum collection made circa 1890. Overlaid with silver and copper and engraved, they have long chap guards and flared swinging buttons. Stamped under buttons with number and maker's initials.

Stone, L. D. California.

Merged with Main & Winchester, 1905. Merged with Keyston Brothers, 1912.

Stos, J. W. Saint Louis, Missouri.

Stamped inside heel band J. W. above STOS.

Strong, Harold. Pecos, Texas, area.

Harold Strong (sometimes spelled Straung) was a Swedish sailor who jumped ship in New York. He finally received his American citizenship after fighting for the United States in World War I. He made spurs in West Texas. He had first gone to Austin, then had ridden horseback to West Texas. He cowboyed for several ranchers in the Pecos area and was a good carpenter and blacksmith. He had his own blacksmith shop in Cottonwood, Texas, in 1920 and then bought a saddle shop in Pecos about 1930. He made spurs prior to owning the saddle shop. Known as "the big Swede," Harold Strong died in the mid-1950s in Big Spring, Texas. He was buried in Anson, Texas, in the Loving family cemetery. He stamped a flying S on his bits and button straps of both spurs or under buttons. Sometimes stamped year by mark. Some styles have a diamond-shaped shank. Strong made unusual gal-leg spurs with the two legs forming a diamond-shaped shank and bits with the leg forming the bottom half of the cheek pieces.

————. England.

Heavy spurs like gun metal. Engraved in silver material. Made in England for American market. Stamped B in a horseshoe on outside of heel band by button and SUPER NEVER RUST on inside of band next to button.

SW Company. New York.

Stamped NEXTOSTEEL by buttons.

TexTan Saddle Company. Yoakum, Texas.

Aluminum spurs.

Thomas, Mark. Alvarado, Texas.

Began making spurs in 1973, making both production spurs and custom orders. Stamped MT.

Trammel Bit & Spur Company. Albany and Haskell, Texas.

Founder Jim Trammel specialized in bits. Contemporary.

Traylor, ————. Houston, Texas, area.

Learned spur making in Texas Penitentiary. It is said that after Traylor died, his cousin made spurs and used his name. No mark.

Troxell, Frank. Nemo, South Dakota.

Gal-leg pattern has silver garters and shoes on bronze legs. FT stamped under button on inside of band.

Tucker, S. H. Gatesville, Texas.

Blacksmith. Iron spurs circa 1920. No mark.

Ulite, ————.

Rowel turned sideways.

Upton, Bud. San Angelo, Texas.

PRCA steer roper and rancher. Name and brand inside heel band of gal-leg spurs made in 1960s.

Vicolette (Dewsbury). Walsall, England.

Products exported to the United States. Curved brass spur. Stamped VICOLETTE on heel band. *See* John Dewsbury & Son.

Vogel, O. A. Sutherlin, Oregon.

A fine steel spur made by Oregon blacksmith Vogel. Stamped O. A. VOGEL SUTHERLIN ORE. on side of shank. Turned up heel bands and 10-point rowels.

Vogt Western Silver, Ltd. Turlock, California.

Stamped VOGT inside cheek piece of bits. Hand-forged and hand-engraved. Silver and gold mounting. Sterling overlay and stainless steel or sterling inlay. Also blued steel spurs. Nickel-plated bits and spurs. Maker of both cowboy and buckaroo bits and spurs.

Warren, Stanley. Lexington, Nebraska.

    Warren became part-time spur maker in 1947 and full-time in 1963. His spurs are a variety of styles with stationary buttons. Using steel from old farm machinery to make many traditional cowboy style spurs, he mounts them with gold, silver, copper, and brass. Two-piece spurs. No engraving.

Weast, W. N. Silverton, Texas.

    Worked with Bass in Quitaque, Texas. Shank diamond-shaped with cut-out. Stamped under swinging button: MADE BY/W. N. WEAST/SILVERTON/TEX.

————, San Angelo, Texas.

    Stamped WIKE.

Wroe, W. T., and Sons. Austin, Texas.

    Saddle maker. Iron spurs with rounded heel bands and shanks and double buttons. Stamped on side by buttons.

Wymer, George. Gatesville, Texas.

    Blacksmith. Well known for his branding irons as well as his plain steel spurs. Made most of the branding irons exhibited at Texas State Fair during centennial exhibits of 1935 and 1936. Died circa 1964. No mark.

Zimmer, ————. Pecos, Texas.

    A blacksmith in Pecos before Harold Strong. Also owned a livery stable and hardware store there. Stamped ZIMMER on side of heel band in front of button.

Notes

Introduction

1. Dick Halliday, "The Romantic Saga of the Spur," *Cattleman* 15 (Jan., 1929): 26–28.

2. Captain Flack, *The Texan Ranger, or Real Life in a Backwoods* (London: Darton and Co., [1866]), p. 305.

3. Brantz Mayer, *Mexico As It Was and As It Is* (New York: J. Winchester, New World Press, 1854), p. 163; Harry Ingerton, typescript of interview with J. Evetts Haley, Amarillo, Tex., June 19, 1937, Harry Ingerton interview file, Nita Stewart Haley Memorial Library, Midland, Tex., p. 20.

4. Ella Bird Dumont, "The True Life Story of Ella Bird Dumont," Tommy J. Boley, Master's thesis, University of Texas, 1963, p. 115.

5. Edgar Rye, "Frontier Reminiscence," Albany (Tex.) *News,* Jan. 30, 1891.

6. R. H. Crosby, typescript of interview with J. Evetts Haley, Kenna, N. Mex., Aug. 4, 1937, R. H. Crosby interview file, Nita Stewart Haley Memorial Library, Midland, Tex., p. 12.

7. Marc Simmons and Frank Turley, *Southwestern Colonial Ironwork: The Spanish Blacksmithing Tradition from Texas to California* (Santa Fe: Museum of New Mexico Press, 1980), p. 110; Philip Ashton Rollins, *The Cowboy* (rev. ed., New York: Ballantine Books, 1973), pp. 99, 106–107.

8. Ingerton interview transcript, p. 16.

9. Rollins, *Cowboy,* p. 99.

10. Edward H. Bohlin, *Catalog of "The World's Finest" Riding Equipment, Riding Accessories and Silver and Leather Goods* (Los Angeles: Privately printed, 1930), p. 4.

11. W. R. (Wallie) Boone, *W. R. (Wallie) Boone Catalogue No. 3* (San Angelo: Privately printed, [ca. 1936], p. 1.

12. Francis Bayers Hamm quoted in Dwight W. Huber, "Adolph Bayers, Texas Spur Maker," pt. 3, *Spur Collectors' Quarterly* 2 (Winter, 1985): 7. Although Bayers did use electrically powered buffers, punches, and other labor-saving devices acquired from the shops of J. R. McChesney and Nocona Boot Company, he never substituted mechanization for craftsmanship, particularly in the refining and decorating of the basic spur body, nor did he employ other workers.

Chapter 1, Spurs

1. Dwight Huber, interview with author, Canyon, Tex., Apr. 28, 1983; Tom Reagan, interview with author, Beeville, Tex., Mar., 1983; spur collections of Dwight Huber, Canyon, Tex., Tom Reagan, Beeville, Tex., and Lloyd Mitchell, Gatesville, Tex.; Dwight Huber, "Spurs: An Illustrated History," pt. 1, *Western Horseman,* Jan., 1979, p. 14.

2. "The Mexican Spur: A Reflection on History of the Charro Trappings," *Mexican Charro,* May–June, 1956, p. 92; spur collections of Huber, Reagan, Mitchell, and Pattie.

3. Spur collections of Huber, Reagan, Mitchell, and Pattie.

4. Dwight Huber, "Spurs: An Illustrated History," pt. 2, *Western Horseman,* Feb., 1979, pp. 15–17; spur collections of Huber, Mitchell, Wheat.

5. Catalogs of Denver Dry Goods Co., Denver, 1920, 1921, 1930; Duhamel Co., Rapid City, S. Dak., *Catalog no. 3* (1927); Otto F. Ernst, Inc., Sheridan, Wyo., *Catalog no. 13* (1930); Al. Furstnow Saddlery Company, Miles City, Mont., *Illustrated Catalog No. 31* (ca. 1930).

6. *Buermann's Saddlery Hardware Catalogue No. 35,* p. 87: picture of "Patent Leg Pattern Bits" all marked PATENTED or BUERMANN'S PATENT with the date of the Gilham design, PAT. DEC 28 86, stamped inside the cheek piece.

7. Pascal M. Kelly, interview with author, Oceanside, Calif., June 28, 1973.

8. Arthur C. Ansley, *Manufacturing Methods and Processes*, pp. 1–6.

9. Dan Reebel, ed., *Manufacturing Methods: ABC of Iron and Steel*, pp. 387–97; Rex Miller and Thomas J. Morrisey, *Metal Technology*, pp. 146–51.

Chapter 3, August Buermann

1. Ellis R. Meeker, comp., *New Jersey: A Historical, Commercial and Industrial Review*, p. 244.

2. *Buermann's Saddlery Hardware, Catalog no. 35* (1922); *U.S. Census Records*. National Archives, Federal Records Center, 1900 Codex, vol. 19, ed. 86, sheet 1, line 9; Frederick W. Ricord, *Biographical Encyclopedia of Successful Men of New Jersey*, vol. 1, pp. 143–44; Meeker, *New Jersey*, p. 244; *Newark Evening News*, Nov. 2, 1928, p. 19. Joseph Atkinson, *The History of New Jersey*, states that the founders of Crane & Co. on Mechanic Street, pioneers of the saddlery hardware trade in the city, started business about 1834. Buermann was also listed, but not Barclay.

3. Ricord, *Biographical Encyclopedia*, 1:143; Meeker, *New Jersey*, p. 244; *Newark Evening News*, Nov. 2, 1928, p. 19.

4. Newark, New Jersey, City Directory, 1879, p. 133, 1880, p. 152; Barbara S. Irwin, reference librarian, New Jersey Historical Society, to Jane Pattie, May 3, 1978; *The Manufacturers of the United States for Domestic & Foreign Trade*, p. 204. By 1901, August Buermann was one of sixteen saddlery hardware manufacturers in Newark, and in 1906 he was one of thirteen listed in *The Industrial Directory of New Jersey*, comp. William Stainsby, 1901 and 1906.

5. Meeker, *New Jersey*, p. 244.

6. *Newark Evening News*, Nov. 2, 1928.

7. *Newark Evening News*, Sept. 13, 1961, and Mar. 9, 1920.

8. Meeker, *New Jersey*, p. 244.

9. Patent and trademark information from U.S. Patent Office, Washington, D.C.

10. *Buermann's Saddlery Hardware, Catalog no. 35.*

11. Ibid.; catalogs from Charles P. Shipley Saddlery and Mercantile Co., nos. 19, 23; Miles City Saddlery Co., no. 29; Al. Furstnow Saddlery Co., nos. 31 (ca. 1930), 32 (ca. 1931); Aniser Mercantile Co. (1922); Denver Dry Goods Co. (1920, 1920–21, 1921, 1930); Dodson Saddlery Co., no. 23; Fiss, Doerr & Carroll Horse Co. (1906); and Sears, Roebuck & Co., *Special Vehicle, Harness, and Saddlery Catalog* (1897, 1901). Representative spurs may also be found in the collections of Lyle and Jane Pat-

tie, Lloyd Mitchell, the estate of O. R. Huff, Tom Reagan, Jim Wheat, Dwight Huber, Jack Thomas, Bob Cantrell, and the Cowboy Hall of Fame, Oklahoma City.

12. Charles P. Shipley Saddlery and Mercantile Co., 1913.

13. *New York Times*, Sept. 28, 1876; *Buermann's Saddlery Hardware, Catalog no. 35;* Meeker, *New Jersey*, p. 244; Ricord, *Biographical Encyclopedia*, 1:143. The Centennial Awards were twenty-eight groups of awards from 125 judges—bronze medals to exhibitors of similar articles, not ranked against each others.

14. P. M. Kelly, interview with author, Oceanside, Calif., June 28, 1973.

15. *Buermann's Saddlery Hardware, Catalog no. 35.* The trademark "Dom Pedro" was issued to August Buermann by the Patent Office. Dom Pedro was emperor of Brazil, who visited the United States during the 1876 centennial year (Donald E. Worcester, *Brazil: From Colony to World Power*, pp. 129–30.)

16. J. H. Flachmeier, *Pioneer Austin Notables*, 2:82–85, copy held by Cowboy Hall of Fame, Oklahoma City; Kathryn Patterson (Petmecky's granddaughter) to J. Evetts Haley, Aug. 28, 1939, Nita Stewart Haley Library.

17. N. Howard (Jack) Thorp, in collaboration with Neil M. Clark, *Pardner of the Wind*, p. 43. Thorp tells of writing "Little Joe, the Wrangler" on an old paper bag with a pencil stub in 1898, as he sat by a campfire nearly ten years after the trail drive he describes in the song. In the version he quotes, there is no mention of an O. K. spur, only "his spurs had rung the knell. . . ." Austin E. Fife and Alta S. Fife, in their *Cowboy and Western Songs*, p. 214, write that the version of "Little Joe, the Wrangler" presented in this volume includes the stanza about the O. K. spur. Fife and Fife credit this version to Thorp in his *Songs of the Cowboy*, pp. 9–11.

18. *Buermann's Saddlery Hardware, Catalog no. 35; North & Judd Manufacturing Co., Catalog no. 82* (1909), *Catalog no. 87* (19   ); U.S. Patent Office records; "Mystery Spur . . . The O. K.," *Western Horseman*, 33, no. 12 (Dec., 1968): 112–13.

19. Spurs from the collections of Lloyd Mitchell and O. R. Huff.

Chapter 4, North & Judd

1. The early history of North & Judd comes from the following three sources (from the collection of Ralph L. Emerson, Jr., of Newington, Conn.): "The History of North & Judd Manufacturing Co.," New Britain, Conn.,

Nov., 1925; *New Britain Record,* May 11, 1866; and Elbridge M. Wightman, comp., *Brief History of North & Judd Mfg. Company, New Britain, Conn.* (a report compiled in 1945). Wightman had been secretary of the company since 1898; he had been an employee since 1882.

2. Telephone interview, Nov. 11, 1983.

3. Wightman, *Brief History.*

4. Moody's Manual of Investments, 1929, p. 366.

5. Ibid., 1929, p. 366, and 1935, p. 754; Wightman, *History of North & Judd.*

6. Muter interview; *Moody's Industrial Manual,* 1983, vol. 1, A-I, p. 1568.

7. Muter interview.

8. Ibid.

9. North & Judd Mfg. Co., *Anchor Brand Harness Hardware, Catalog No. 83* (1914).

10. Ralph Emerson, Jr., telephone interview with author, Newington, Conn., Nov. 11, 1983; North & Judd Mfg. Co., *"Anchor Brand" Saddlery Hardware, Price List no. 35* (1886–87); North & Judd, *Catalog no. 83* (1914) and *Catalog no. 87,* collection of Bob Taylor of Santa Fe, N.Mex.; August Buermann Mfg. Co., *Buermann's Saddlery Hardware, Catalog no. 35,* collection of Lloyd Mitchell, Gatesville, Tex.; Muter telephone interview.

11. U.S. Patent Office, Trademark Registration No. 88,465, Registered Sept. 24, 1912, by August Buermann Manufacturing Company. Renewed by North & Judd Manufacturing Co.

12. North & Judd catalogs in collection of Ralph L. Emerson, Jr., Newington, Conn.

13. *North & Judd, Star Steel Silver, Catalog no. 93* (1953), in the collection of Panhandle-Plains Historical Museum Research Center, Canyon, Tex. In the collection of Ralph Emerson, Jr., are a pair of spurs marked ELDONIAN STAINLESS STEEL, with a star and a hardware tag on which is printed "Eldonian STAINLESS STEEL RIDING HARDWARE MANUFACTURED BY GEORGE SHELDON LTD., WALSALL, ENGLAND. Distributed exclusively in the U.S.A. by NORTH & JUDD MFG. CO., NEW BRITAIN, CONNECTICUT." The trademark includes a star. The North & Judd and Eldonian partnership was short-lived.

14. North & Judd, *Catalog no. 83;* Muter interview.

15. Copy of patent in Emerson collection; Emerson interview; Muter interview.

Chapter 5, John Robert McChesney

1. Statement written by Robert McChesney, Ardmore, Okla., Jan. 9, 1967, in files of the Cowboy Hall of Fame and Western Heritage Center, Oklahoma City.

2. Clippings, *Pauls Valley Enterprise,* Jan. 12, 1928.

3. Edna (Mrs. T. C.) McChesney, interview with author, Pauls Valley, Okla., May 12, 1983.

4. Robert McChesney statement. He writes, "By 1887, they moved to what is now known as Broken Bow, Oklahoma, but at that time it was known as Indian Territory." A letter from Dean Foster, president of the McCurtain County Historical Society, to author May 19, 1983, states that Broken Bow was established in 1911 by Choctaw Lumber Company.

The settlement of Broken Arrow south of Tulsa seems more likely to have been the site of McChesney's blacksmith shop. Tulsa was founded in 1882 as a siding of the Atlantic & Pacific Railroad and soon became a great cattle shipping point. Broken Arrow was about 15 miles from Tulsa, within walking distance, while Broken Bow was nearer 150 miles and through some very rough country. No freighter would have hauled the shop and equipment to Broken Bow for fifty cents. Broken Arrow was also in ranching country, while Broken Bow is in a lumbering area. The stories concerning the happenings in Indian Territory are based on Robert McChesney's statement, except for the Belle Starr story, note 3.

5. Robert McChesney statement.

6. A. Morton Smith, *The First 100 Years in Cooke County,* pp. 103–106.

7. Michael Collins, *Cooke County, Texas: Where the South and West Meet,* p. 45; Smith, *First 100 Years,* p. 146; Kirby McPherson, interview with author, Santa Fe, N.Mex., Nov. 20, 1982; Bob Taylor, interview with author, Houston, Mar. 16, 1983.

8. Clinton McPherson, interview with author, Valley View, Tex., Oct. 10, 1983; clipping, *Pauls Valley Enterprise,* Jan. 12, 1928.

9. Smith, *First 100 Years,* pp. 96–97, 138; Robert McChesney statement. In a letter dated Mar. 3, 1989 (Angleton, Tex.), Lewis W. Browning wrote: "My father, N. C. Browning, loved horses and hated to see them treated badly. Dad would not make at any price a severe spur or severe bridle bit. He started working with spurs in Gainesville, Tex. around 1907. Most spur orders came by mail or were picked up by his boss (J. R. McChesney) who rode 'Star Route' [mail delivery] where he saw cowboys and had his samples with him. He took down their orders as to plain buttons or swinging buttons, whether raised or drop shank, diameter of the rowel and number of points. My Dad did the engraving, also. The first shop was in 1/2 of a horse-drawn

streetcar body and the only workers were the owner and my Dad. The business grew and Sears wanted to sell their product. Sears asked to buy their seconds. Sears was told, 'No dice! We do not produce seconds.'"

10. Kirby McPherson interview; Smith, *First 100 Years,* p. 27.

11. Clinton McPherson interview; *J. R. McChesney Spurs & Bits Catalog,* [1906], Gainesville, Tex., in Cowboy Hall of Fame Collection.

12. Enid Justin (Nocona, Tex.), telephone interview with author, May 15, 1978; Edna (Mrs. Robert) McChesney, telephone interview, May 15, 1978; Enid Justin to O. R. Huff, Apr. 16, 1971; Jack Thomas, "A History of the Texas Spur," pt. I, *Western Horseman,* Aug. 1973, p. 86.

13. Kirby McPherson interview.

14. Kirby McPherson interview.

15. Ibid.; Smith, *First 100 Years,* p. 45; Collins, *Cooke County,* p. 45.

16. Clipping, *Pauls Valley Enterprise,* Jan. 12, 1928; Warranty Deed, vol. 5, p. 316, Deed Records of Garvin County, Okla.; Joe Willard, interview with author, Pauls Valley, Okla., May 12, 1983.

17. P. M. Kelly, interview with author, Oceanside, Calif., Aug. 1, 1972; Willard interview.

18. Willard interview.

19. Robert McChesney statement.

20. Willard interview.

21. Ibid.; Virgie Castro, interview with author, Pauls Valley, Okla., May 28, 1983; Jewell Panell, interview with author, Pauls Valley, Okla., May 28, 1983; Van Sparks (Pauls Valley, Okla.), telephone interview with author, May 28, 1983; Edna McChesney, interview.

22. Willard interview; clipping, Jan. 12, 1928, *Pauls Valley Enterprise.*

23. Sheriff's Deed, vol. 171, p. 470, Deed Records of Garvin County, Okla.

24. Justin interview; Enid Justin to O. R. Huff; Adolph Bayers, interview, with author, Truscott, Tex., Mar. 6, 1972; Edna McChesney interview.

25. McChesney *Catalog,* [1906], Charles P. Shipley Saddlery & Mercantile Co., Kansas City, Mo., *Catalog no. 23;* Denver Dry Goods Co., *Catalog,* Denver, (1920, 1921); Dodson Saddlery Company, Dallas, Tex., *Catalog no. 23;* Padgitt Bros. Manufacturers & Jobbers, Dallas, Tex., *Catalog no. 83;* G. H. Shoellkopf Saddlery Company, Dallas, Tex., *Catalog no. 25,* 1925.

In "A History of the Texas Spur," Jack Thomas says that McChesney began to receive so many orders from California in 1906, possibly because of a shortage of products after the San Francisco earthquake and fire, that he made a trip to the West Coast to study the market. He went by ship from Galveston through the Panama Canal to California. The ornate silver-inlaid bits and spurs were strictly hand-made and would not fit McChesney's production methods, so he wisely returned to Texas and his own lucrative business.

26. Kirby McPherson interview.

Chapter 6, P. M. Kelly

1. P. M. Kelly, tape recording to author, Oceanside, Calif., May 19, 1975.

2. Pascal M. Kelly, interview with author, Oceanside, Calif., Dec. 1, 1972.

3. Ibid. In a letter (July 26, 1988) to Marcia Preston, editor of *Persimmon Hill,* A. P. Hays wrote, "The first Kelly Bros. spurs were marked on one side of the shank, as well as by the button." Hays enclosed a photo of two pairs of Kelly Bros. spurs marked in this manner.

4. Pascal M. Kelly, interview with author, Oceanside, Calif., Aug. 1, 1972; Jack Thomas, "A History of the Texas Spur," pt. 1, *Western Horseman,* Aug. 1973, p. 86.

5. Patent Number 1,397,966 filed by Pascal M. Kelly, Dalhart, Tex., Mar. 23, 1921, and issued Nov. 22, 1921. All three styles of buttons are pictured in *Catalog no. 11* (1928) of R. J. Andrew & Son, San Angelo, Tex.; all bits and spurs marked KELLY BROS. Spurs in Lloyd Mitchell collection.

6. Pascal M. Kelly, interview with author, Oceanside, Calif., Sept. 13, 1972.

7. Kelly interview, Dec. 1, 1972.

8. Kelly interview, Aug. 1, 1972.

9. Ibid.; Hettie Vititoe Kelly, interview with author, El Paso, Tex., Aug. 15, 1972; C. M. Roberts, "P. M. Kelly & Sons, Manufacturers," *Western Horseman,* May, 1960, p. 78.

10. Kelly interview, Aug. 1, 1972. The 1920 *Dalhart, Texas, City Directory* lists "Pascal Kelly, prop. of Kelly Bros.; Mgr. Kelly & Company, mfgs. of Kelly's Hot Ball Engines, 318 Denrock Ave. and 322 Conlan Avenue. Grady R. Kelly, Foreman Kelly Bros., 401 Conlan." Also "Kelly Bros., P. M. Kelly prop., Mfg. hand-forged bits and spurs, 318 Denrock." One of Kelly's Hot Ball Engines is exhibited in the XIT Museum, Dalhart, Texas.

11. *P. M. Kelly & Sons, Catalog no. 64;* Kelly interview, Sept. 13, 1972.

12. Kelly interview, Sept. 13, 1972; Hettie Kelly to author, May 14, 1973; "P. M. Kelly & Sons," *El Paso Times,* May 4, 1947.

13. Kelly interview, Dec. 1, 1972; *Denver Post,* July 2, 1973. An undated advertisement

for Kelly's in *Western Horseman* states, "After June 30th, 1965, all correspondence and orders pertaining to bits and spurs must be directed to Crockett and Renalde . . . Denver, Colorado."

14. Kelly interview, Aug. 1, 1972.
15. Ibid.
16. Hettie Kelly to author, May 14, 1973.

Chapter 7, Oscar Crockett

1. Hazel A. Crockett, interview with author, Boulder, Colo., May 16, 1975.
2. Oscar Crockett, "Just a Word with You," in Crockett Bit & Spur Co., *Catalog no. 11,* Kansas City, Mo. (1928); Miles City Saddlery Co., Miles City, Mont., unnumbered catalog, 1920s; Jack Thomas to author, Fallbrook, Calif., May 27, 1975; Hazel Crockett interview.
3. *Crockett Catalog* no. 12.
4. Hazel Crockett interview; *Crockett Catalog no. 12.*
5. Chas. P. Shipley Saddlery & Mercantile Co., Kansas City, Mo., *Catalog no. 16* (1917).
6. *Crockett Catalog no. 12;* Pascal M. Kelly, interview with author, Oceanside, Calif., Aug. 1, 1972; Hazel Crockett interview.
7. Pascal M. Kelly interview; Crockett Saddle & Harness Co., Kansas City, Mo., *Catalog no. 1* (n.d.); Crockett Bit & Spur Co., Lenexa Kans., *Catalog no. 14* (1934); Crockett Bit & Spur Co., Boulder, Colo., *Catalog no. 50* (1950); Hazel Crockett interview.
8. Hazel Crockett interview. The 1930 catalog of Miles City Saddlery Company, Miles City, Mont., advertised two styles of Crockett Stainless Steel spurs and five styles of "Crockett's 'Feather-Light' Airplane Metal Spurs., Rust-proof and Tarnishproof One-Piece heel bands and shanks." The spurs advertised in the 1932 Miles City Saddlery Company catalog were all "Crockett Hand Forged Steel Spurs."
9. Hazel Crockett interview.
10. Nicholas J. Nagle, "Ricardo in Metal," *Western Horseman* (undated tear sheet), p. 30.
11. Pascal M. Kelly interview: "I never saw a harder working fellow than Oscar Crockett. He had more determination than any other fellow I ever saw. He was certainly due credit for being a good worker. After James Renalde bought the Crockett Bit & Spur Company from Mrs. Crockett in 1951, Renalde told me, 'They had enough aluminum bits in inventory to be worth what I had to give for the business.'"
12. Hazel Crockett interview.
13. *Denver Post,* July 2, 1973; Al Gabriella, interview with author, Boulder, Colo., May 16, 1975.

14. Gabriella interview.
15. Crockett & Kelly, Inc., Broomfield, Colo., *Catalog no. 180.*

Chapter 8, The Shops of Bischoff and Shipley

1. G. A. Bischoff & Co., Gainesville, Tex., *Catalog no. 1* (Sept., 1911), reprint by Martin Enterprises, Clovis, N. Mex.
2. Pascal M. Kelly, interview with author, Oceanside, Calif., Aug. 1, 1972.
3. 1900 Census Records, Cooke County, Tex.; Paul J. Schad to author, Gainesville, Tex., Nov. 7, 1983.
4. A. Morton Smith, *The First 100 Years in Cooke County,* p. 142.
5. Clinton McPherson, interview with author, Valley View, Tex., Oct. 10, 1983.
6. Smith, *First 100 Years,* pp. 142, 161; Shipley, *Catalog no. 16.*
7. McPherson interview.
8. Bischoff & Co., *Catalog no. 1;* Chas. P. Shipley Saddlery & Mercantile Co., Kansas City, *Catalog no. 16* (ca. 1917), p. 10.
9. *Gainesville Daily Register,* Feb. 28, 1916.
10. *Gainesville Daily Register,* May 16, 1944.
11. Paul J. Schad (Gainesville, Tex.), telephone interview with author, Nov. 5, 1983.
12. *Gainesville Daily Register,* Oct. 15, 1954.
13. Charles P. Shipley II to author, undated, 1974; *Men of Affairs in Greater Kansas City, 1912* (Kansas City, Mo.: Kansas City Press Club, n.d.).
14. P. M. Kelly interview, Aug. 1, 1972.
15. Shipley *Catalog no. 16,* pp. 15, 17; Shipley *Catalog no. 17,* p. 105; Shipley *Catalog no. 18.*
16. P. M. Kelly interview.
17. Charles P. Shipley II to author, Prairie View, Kansas, undated, 1974; *Kansas City Times,* Sept. 14, 1943; *Kansas City Star,* Jan. 16, 1927.

Chapter 9, Robert Lincoln Causey

1. Mary Causey Anglin, interview with author, Safford, Ariz., Apr. 15, 1983; R. L. Causey family papers, in possession of Mary Causey Anglin, Safford, Ariz.; Certificate of Death of Robert L. Causey, State of Arizona.
2. J. Evetts Haley, *George W. Littlefield, Texan,* pp. 157–63; J. Evetts Haley, *The XIT Ranch of Texas and the Early Days of the Llano Estacado,* pp. 45–46, 63.
3. Anglin interview; V. H. Whitlock, Causey's nephew, states that Causey learned the

blacksmith trade from his father, G. W. Causey (V. H. Whitlock, *Cowboy Life on the Llano Estacado*, p. 110).

4. Whitlock, *Cowboy Life*, p. 110.

5. Ibid., p. 114; Anglin interview.

6. Anglin interview; Whitlock, *Cowboy Life*, p. 111.

7. Ol' Waddy, "Bits & Spurs," *Western Horseman*, Nov., 1952, p. 31; Whitlock, *Cowboy Life*, p. 111.

8. Whitlock, *Cowboy Life*, p. 110; Ol' Waddy, "Yesterday's Cow-Town Blacksmith," *Western Horseman*, Apr., 1962, p. 34.

9. Ol' Waddy, "Yesterday's Blacksmith," p. 34; Anglin interview.

10. Anglin interview; Whitlock, *Cowboy Life*, p. 112; Ol' Waddy, "Bits & Spurs."

11. Ol' Waddy, "Bits & Spurs"; Anglin interview.

12. Whitlock, *Cowboy Life*, p. 112.

13. Anglin interview.

14. Ibid.

15. Ibid.

16. Newspaper clipping, Pico, Calif., 1932, Causey family papers.

17. Causey death certificate; Anglin interview; clipping dated Feb. 12, 1937, Causey family papers.

Chapter 10, *Joe Bianchi and the Victoria Shank*

1. Spurs in collection of Jack Thomas, Fallbrook, Calif.; Tom Reagan, interview with author, Beeville, Tex., Mar. 10, 1983.

2. *In Memory of Mr. Joe (Joseph) Bianchi*, compiled Apr. 15, 1974, from information furnished by Joe Bianchi's nephew, C. J. Fossati, by the Sisters of the Incarnate Word and Blessed Sacrament, Victoria, Tex. (Bianchi files, Bob Taylor, Santa Fe).

3. Raymond E. Maher, "Forty Years at the Forge," *Cattleman*, Aug., 1949, p. 24.

4. Bianchi files, Bob Taylor, Santa Fe; Sidney Weisiger Biography File, Local History Collection, Victoria College, Victoria, Tex. (courtesy of R. W. Shook, Victoria College).

5. Maher, "Forty Years"; Bob Taylor, interview with author, Houston, Apr. 20, 1983. Fossati states, "Paul opened a blacksmith shop which was located on Juan Linn at Bridge. Later, Mr. Joe left the farm and joined Paul in the shop to learn the trade. The business was then known as Bianchi Brothers Blacksmith Shop. In 1906 Joe opened his own shop on South William Street."

6. Marriage license, Marriage Records of Victoria County, Tex., vol. 6, p. 283; Maher,

"Forty Years"; Weisiger files; Bianchi files; Taylor interview.

7. Reagan interview.

8. "Forty Years."

9. Joe Bianchi *Catalog C*, Panhandle-Plains Historical Museum; Bianchi *Catalog E*, Jane Pattie collection; Bianchi *Catalog G*, Bob Taylor collection.

10. Tom Regan spur collection, Beeville; Dwight Huber spur collection, Canyon, Tex.; Dwight Huber, interview with author, Canyon Tex., Apr. 28, 1983.

11. Pascal M. Kelly, interview with author, Oceanside, Calif., June 28, 1973.

12. Duval Davidson, interview with author, Fort Worth, Oct. 8, 1973; Emil Marks, interview with author, Barker, Tex., Apr. 15, 1969. Davidson was a descendant of the prominent Traylor family. Well-known South Texas cattleman Emil Marks owned a pair of Traylor spurs that stayed buckled on his boots even when he took his boots off.

13. Reagan interview.

14. Clipping, *Victoria Advocate*, May 30, 1949; *In Memory*; Death Certificate, Victoria County Records, Victoria, Tex.

15. Huber interview; spur in Lloyd Mitchell collection.

Chapter 11, *The Boones*

1. Pate Boone, interview with author, Christoval, Tex., Feb. 4, 1975; Pecos Pate Boone, *The Boone Boys, Frontiersmen, and Their Great Wild West Show*, p. 6.

2. Boone, *Boone Boys*, pp. 6, 7–8; Bob Boone, interview with author, San Diego, Calif., May 28, 1973.

3. Pate Boone interview.

4. Bob Boone interview.

5. Pate Boone interview; Boone, *Boone Boys*, pp. 25–30.

6. Pate Boone interview; Boone, *Boone Boys*, pp. 25–30.

7. Boone, *Boone Boys*, p. 33.

8. Pate Boone interview.

9. Ibid.; Boone, *Boone Boys*, p. 50.

10. Marisue Potts, Motley County Historical Commission, to author, Floydada, Tex., June 4, 1989. In Pate Boone's interview he said, "Wallie blacksmithed at Lubbock and Amarillo before he had his spur factory in San Angelo." Motley County is northeast of Lubbock, and it is possible that Pate meant the Lubbock area.

11. Pate Boone interview; Pascal M. Kelly, interview with author, Oceanside, Calif., Sept. 13, 1972.

12. *San Angelo Standard Times,* Nov. 24, 1944.

13. Ibid., Nov. 21, 1945; Tom Reagan, interview with author, Beeville, Tex., Mar. 10, 1983.

14. Death Certificate, Howard County, Tex.

15. Kelly interview.

16. Death Certificate, Tom Green County, Tex.

17. Dee Boone, interview with author, Henryetta, Okla., May 1, 1973.

18. Ibid.

19. Ibid.; Pate Boone interview.

20. Dee Boone interview.

21. Bob Boone interview.

22. Blanch Boone Gollaher, interview with author, San Diego, Calif., May 28, 1973. Gollaher is Bob Boone's daughter.

23. Bob Boone interview.

24. This feature was actually not new. It is seen on some Spanish spurs as well as Moroccan spurs.

Chapter 12, J. O. Bass

1. Orville Howard, "Tulia Spur Maker," *Cattleman,* Nov., 1970.

2. J. O. Bass, Jr. (Plainview, Tex.), telephone interview with author, June 1, 1978.

3. Dwight Huber, interview with author, Canyon, Tex., Apr. 28, 1983.

4. Bass interview; spurs in Mitchell collection and in Huff collection.

5. Huber interview.

6. In "Tulia Spur Maker," Howard states that Nolan Jones was Bass's partner, but J. O. Bass, Jr., says that Jones worked for his father.

7. Howard, "Tulia Spur Maker."

8. Huber interview.; J. O. Bass *Catalog* (1912), Panhandle-Plains Historical Museum Research Center, Canyon, Tex.

9. Huber interview; Grubb, quoted in Huber interview.

10. Huber interview; Bass *Catalog* (1912).

11. Huber says, "I've seen five different Bass catalogs, from about 1909 through 1914."

12. Bass interview.

13. Certificate of Death, Cert. #6299, Falls County, Tex.

Chapter 13, Jess Hodge

1. Louie Lehne (Menard, Tex.), telephone interview with author, Dec. 10, 1983; Frances Fish (Menard, Tex.), telephone interview with author, Aug. 17, 1977; *Menard County History, an Anthology* (Menard, Tex.: Menard County Historical Society, 1982), p. 38.

2. *Menard News,* Mar. 12, 1953; Fish interview.

3. Lehne interview; John Treadwell (Fort McKavett, Tex.), telephone interview with author, Dec. 10, 1983; Fish interview; Lynell Wheless (Menard, Tex.), telephone interviews with author, Dec. 10, 1983, Jan. 5, 1984.

4. *Menard News,* Mar. 12, 1953.

5. Lehne interview.

6. Fish interview.

7. Juanita Buntyn (Sonora, Tex.), telephone interview with author, Dec. 10, 1983; Fish interview.

Chapter 14, E. F. Blanchard

1. This chapter is based on an interview with Edward Fred Blanchard, Yucca, Ariz., June 1, 1973.

2. *Blanchard Spurs,* brochure, Yucca, Ariz., ca. 1970, in Pattie collection.

3. See N. Porter Company, Phoenix, Ariz., *Porters Saddles and Saddle Accessories, Catalog no. 38,* p. 31, in Panhandle-Plains Historical Museum Research Center.

4. *Blanchard Spurs; Porters Catalog no. 38,* p. 31.

5. Certificate of Death of Edward Fred Blanchard, State of Arizona.

6. Mrs. Arthur H. Blanchard to author, Cherry Valley, Calif., May 21, 1978.

Chapter 15, Adolph Bayers

1. This chapter is based on an interview with Adolph R. Bayers, Truscott, Tex., on Mar. 6, 1972.

2. Statement written by Robert McChesney, Ardmore, Okla., Jan. 9, 1967, Cowboy Hall of Fame and Western Heritage Center, Oklahoma City; Enid Justin (Nocona Boot Company) to O. R. Huff, Nocona, Tex., Apr. 16, 1971; Enid Justin (Nocona, Tex.), telephone interview with author, May 15, 1978.

3. A. R. Bayers Collection, Panhandle-Plains Historical Museum Research Center, Canyon, Tex.

4. C. E. Miller, interview with author, Mason, Tex., Feb. 12, 1972.

Bibliography

Books

Adams, Ramon R. *The Old Time Cowhand.*
New York: Macmillan Company, 1961.
———. *Western Words: A Dictionary of the
American West.* Norman: University of
Oklahoma Press, 1968.
Ansley, Arthur C. *Manufacturing Methods
and Processes.* Philadelphia: Chilton Com-
pany, 1968.
Atkinson, Joseph. *The History of Newark, New
Jersey.* Newark, N.J.: William B. Guild,
1878.
Blumenstein, Lynn. *Wishbook 1865: Relic Iden-
tification for the Year 1865.* Salem, Ore-
gon: Old Time Bottle Publishing Com-
pany, 1968.
Boone, Pecos Pate. *The Boone Boys, Frontiers-
men, and Their Great Wild West Show.*
Christoval, Tex.: Privately printed,
1976.
Branch, Douglas. *The Cowboy and His Inter-
preters.* New York: D. Appleton and Com-
pany, 1926.
Brereton, J. M., *The Horse in War.* New York:
Arco Publishing Company, 1976.
Coggins, Jack. *The Fighting Man.* Garden
City, New York: Doubleday & Company,
Inc., 1966.
Collins, Michael. *Cooke County, Texas: Where
the South and West Meet.* Cooke County
Heritage Society, 1981.
Directory—Newark Made Goods. Board of
Trade of the City of Newark, N.J., 1913.
Dobie, J. Frank. *The Longhorns.* New York:
Bramhall House, 1951.
Emmett, Chris. *Shanghai Pierce: A Fair Like-
ness.* Norman: University of Oklahoma
Press, 1953.
Fife, Austin E., and Alta S. Fife. *Cowboy and*

Western Songs. New York: Clarkson N.
Potter, 1969.
Foster-Harris, William. *The Look of the Old
West.* New York: Viking Press, 1955.
Gard, Wayne. *The Chisholm Trail.* Norman:
University of Oklahoma Press, 1954.
Haley, J. Evetts. *George W. Littlefield, Texan.*
Norman: University of Oklahoma Press,
1943.
———. *The XIT Ranch of Texas and the Early
Days of the Llano Estacado.* Norman: Uni-
versity of Oklahoma Press, 1953.
The History of North & Judd Manufacturing Co.
New Britain, Conn.: Privately printed,
Nov. 1925.
In and About New Britain. New Britain, Conn.:
Lewis & Atwell, 1892.
The Industrial Directory of New Jersey, compiled
by William Stainsby. Trenton, N.J.:
Bureau of Statistics of New Jersey, 1901
and 1906.
James, Will. *All in the Day's Riding.* New
York: Charles Scribner's Sons, 1943.
Lord, Francis A. *Civil War Collector's
Encyclopedia.* New York: Castle Books,
1963, 1965.
*Manufacturers of the United States for Domestic
and Foreign Trade.* New York: Armstrong
& Knauer Publishing Co., 1888.
Meeker, Ellis R., comp. *New Jersey: A Histori-
cal, Commercial and Industrial Review.*
Elizabeth, N.J.: Commonwealth Pub-
lishing Co., 1906.
Menard County History: An Anthology. Menard,
Tex.: Menard County Historical Society,
1982.
Men of Affairs in Greater Kansas City, 1912.
Kansas City, Mo.: Kansas City Press
Club.
Miller, Rex, and Thomas J. Morrisey. *Metal*

Technology. New York: Howard W. Sams & Co., 1975.

Moody's Industrial Manual, 1983, Vol. 1, A-I.

Moody's Manual of Investments, 1929, 1935.

Peterson, Harold L. *The Book of the Continental Soldier.* Harrisburg, Penn.: Stackpole Company, 1968.

Pliska, Mary Beth. *A Blacksmith's Aeroplane.* Privately printed, 1965.

Reebel, Dan, ed. *ABC of Iron and Steel,* sixth ed. Cleveland, Ohio: Penton Publishing Company, 1950.

Ricord, Frederick W. *Biographical Encyclopedia of Successful Men of New Jersey,* vol. 1. New York: New Jersey Historical Publishing Co., 1896.

Smith, A. Morton. *The First 100 Years in Cooke County.* San Antonio: Naylor Company, 1976.

Steffen, Randy. *The Horse Soldier, 1776–1943.* Norman: University of Oklahoma Press, 1977.

Thorp, N. Howard ("Jack"). *Songs of the Cowboy.* Estancia, N.Mex.: News Print Shop, 1908.

———, and Neil M. Clark. *Pardner of the Wind.* Lincoln: University of Nebraska Press, 1977.

Tinker, Edward Larocque. *The Horsemen of the Americas.* Austin: University of Texas Press, 1967.

Vernam, Glenn R. *Man on Horseback.* New York: Harper & Row, 1964.

Ward, Faye E. *The Cowboy at Work.* New York: Hastings Hosue, 1958.

Whitlock, V. H. *Cowboy Life on the Llano Estacado.* Norman: University of Oklahoma Press, 1970.

Articles

Ackerman, R. O. "The Spur Story." *Arizona Highways,* Sept., 1952, p. 36.

Ascasubi, Luis de. "The Spur and Its Use." *Western Horseman,* Dec., 1970, p. 66.

"Bits and Spurs." *Western Horseman,* May, 1956, p. 26.

Boykin, John E. "Spurs for Speed." *True,* Apr., 1966, p. 66.

Carroll, John C. "Silver Mounting Spurs." *Western Horseman,* Sept., 1964, p. 55.

Davis, Ray. "Spurs." *Western Horseman,* July, 1970, p. 94.

Dean, Bashford. "Armor for Horse and Man." *Bulletin of the Metropolitan Museum of Art* 19 (Feb., 1924): 38.

———. "A Descriptive Label for Spurs." *Bulletin of the Metropolitan Museum of Art* 11 (Oct., 1916): 217.

———. "Early Gothic Spurs." *Bulletin of the Metropolitan Museum of Art* 21 (May, 1926): 129.

Dean, Frank. "Animated Spur from Old Mexico." *Western Horseman,* June, 1970, p. 82.

Escarcega, Leovigildo, et al. "La Charraria." *Artes de Mexico* (1967).

"Glenn." "Spurs for the Ladies." *Western Horseman,* May, 1959, p. 92.

Hamilton, John. "The Great Horse Stabbers." *Man's Magazine* (undated), p. 38.

Hedgpeth, Don. "Steel on Their Heels." *Western Horseman,* July, 1968, p. 44.

Howard, Orville. "Tulia Spur Maker." *Cattleman,* Nov., 1970, p. 36.

Huber, Dwight W. "Collecting Spurs." *Antique Trader Weekly,* Nov. 1, 1978, pp. 76–77.

———. "The Mexican Spur," part 2. *Spur Collectors' Quarterly* 3 (Winter, 1986): 3, 5–9.

———. "Selected Pairs of Spurs from the Panhandle Plains Collection." *Tack Room Journal,* Nov., 1978, pp. 8–10.

———. "Spur Maker." *Tack Room Journal,* Sept., 1978, pp. 2–4.

———. "Spurs, an Illustrated History," part 1. *Western Horseman,* Jan., 1979, p. 14. Part 2, Feb., 1979, pp. 14–17.

———. "The Western Spur: An American Original." *Tack Room Journal,* May, 1978, pp. 2–5.

Hughes, Pollyanna B. "Knight or Cowboy, Spurs Made the Man!" *Western Horseman,* Oct., 1955, p. 21.

———. "Spurs Made the Man." *Western Horseman,* Oct., 1963.

"Kelly Sells to C and R." *Quarter Horse Journal,* June, 1965, p. 153.

Lindgren, Carl H. "Spurs and Their Use." *Western Horseman,* Oct., 1954, p. 27.

Livingston, Phil. "David Andrews—Bit Maker in the Texas Tradition." *Quarter Horse Journal,* Sept., 1986, p. 116.

Maher, Raymond E. "Forty Years at the Forge." *Cattleman,* Aug., 1949, p. 24.

Merrill, Louis P. "The Spur." *Cattleman,* Sept., 1941, p. 31.

"The Mexican Spur: A Reflection of History on the Charro Trappings." *Mexican Charro,* May–June, 1956, p. 91.

Mizwa, Ted S. "Edward Bohlin, Saddler in Silver." *Western Outfitter,* May, 1976, pp. 31–34.

Mumford, Ron, and Les Garcia. "Silver and Steel." *Western Outfitter,* Aug., 1973, pp. 18–21.

"Mystery Spur . . . The O.K.," *Western Horseman,* Dec., 1968, pp. 112–13.

O'Brien, Sadie. "Bits and Spurs." *Western Horseman,* Jan., 1965, p. 60.

Ol' Waddy. "Yesterday's Cow-Town Blacksmith." *Western Horseman,* Apr., 1962, p. 34.

Porter, Harold. "Western Merchant Pioneers." *Western Outfitter,* May, 1975, p. 20.

Roberts, C. M. "P. M. Kelly & Sons, Manufacturers." *Western Horseman.* May, 1960, p. 78.

Robertson, Wallace I. "Buckaroo Spurs." *Nevada,* Winter, 1973, p. 12.

Steffen, Randy. "Spurs through History." *Western Horseman,* Feb., 1956, p. 10.

Thomas, Jack. "A History of the Texas Spur," part 1. *Western Horseman,* Aug., 1973, p. 86. Part 2, Sept., 1973, p. 4.

"Truly Western," *True West,* Dec., 1970, p. 46. Dec., 1971, p. 69.

Valentry, Duane. "Horse Gear Brings History to Life." *Western Horseman,* Nov., 1967, p. 20.

Catalogs

Amonett, E. T., Saddlery. Roswell, N.Mex., and El Paso, Tex. Unnumbered catalog (1928), Panhandle-Plains Historical Museum Research Center, Canyon.

Andrew, R. J., & Son. San Angelo. Unnumbered catalog (1916), Collection of Lloyd Mitchell, Gatesville. Unnumbered catalog (1928), Panhandle-Plains Historical Museum Research Center, Canyon.

Aniser Mercantile Company. St. Joseph, Mo. Unnumbered catalog (ca. 1922), Panhandle-Plains Historical Museum Research Center, Canyon.

Bass, J. O. Tulia, Tex. *Hand-made Bridle Bits and Spurs.* Unnumbered catalog (1912), Panhandle-Plains Historical Museum Research Center, Canyon.

Bianchi, Joe. Victoria, Tex. *Spurs and Bits.* Catalog C (ca. 1925), Panhandle-Plains Historical Museum Research Center, Canyon; Catalog E (undated), Collection of Lyle and Jane Pattie, Aledo, Tex.; Catalog G (undated), Collection of Bob Taylor, Santa Fe.

Bischoff, G. A., & Co. Gainesville, Tex. Catalog no. 1 (Sept. 1, 1911), reprint, Martin Enterprises, Clovis, N.Mex., Panhandle-Plains Historical Museum Research Center, Canyon.

Blanchard Spurs. Yucca, Ariz. Brochure (ca. 1970), Collection of Lyle and Jane Pattie, Aledo, Tex.

Bohlin Shop. Hollywood, Calif. Unnumbered catalogs (1931, 1937), Panhandle-Plains Historical Museum Research Center, Canyon.

Buermann, August, Mfg. Co., Newark, N.J. *Buermann's Saddlery Hardware.* Catalog no. 35 (1922), Collection of Lloyd Mitchell, Gatesville, Tex.

Carlock, Carl, Saddle Co. Phoenix, Ariz. Catalog no. 48 (ca. 1940), Catalog no. 50 (1942), Panhandle-Plains Historical Museum Research Center, Canyon.

Circle Y Saddlery, Inc. Yoakum, Tex. Catalog no. 9 (undated), Panhandle-Plains Historical Museum Research Center, Canyon.

Colorado Saddlery Company. Denver, Colo. Catalog no. 178 (undated), Panhandle-Plains Historical Museum Research Center, Canyon.

Court's Saddlery Company. Bryan, Tex. Unnumbered catalog (undated), Panhandle-Plains Historical Museum Research Center, Canyon.

Crockett and Kelly. Denver, Colo. *Bits & Spurs by Renalde.* Catalog no. 74 (1975), Catalog no. 75 (undated), Collection of Lyle and Jane Pattie, Aledo, Tex.

Crockett & Kelly, Inc. Broomfield, Colo. Catalog no. 180 (undated), Panhandle-Plains Historical Museum Research Center, Canyon.

Crockett Bit & Spur Co. Boulder, Colo. Catalog no. 49 (ca. 1948), Collection of Lloyd Mitchell, Gatesville, Tex.; Catalog no. 50 (ca. 1949), Panhandle-Plains Historical Museum Research Center, Canyon.

Crockett Bit & Spur Co. Kansas City, Mo. Catalog no. 7 (undated), Collection of Bob Taylor, Santa Fe; Catalog no. 9 (undated), Collection of Jack Thomas, Fallbrook, Calif.; Catalog no. 11 (1928), Panhandle-Plains Historical Museum Research Center, Canyon; Catalog no. 12 (1932), Collection of Bob Taylor, Santa Fe.

Crockett Bit & Spur Co. Lenexa, Kans. Catalog no. 14 (1934), Panhandle-Plains Historical Museum Research Center, Canyon.

Crockett Bit & Spur Co., owned by James Renalde. Boulder, Colo. Catalog no. 53 (ca. 1951), Panhandle-Plains Historical Museum Research Center, Canyon.

Crockett Saddle & Harness Co. Kansas City, Mo. Catalog no. 1 (undated), Collection of Bob Taylor, Santa Fe.

Denver Dry Goods Co. Denver, Colo. (1920, 1920–21, Spring–Summer, 1931, Fall–Winter, 1935–36), Collection of Lloyd Mitchell, Gatesville, Tex.; (Spring–Summer, 1938), Panhandle-Plains Historical Museum Research Center, Canyon.

Dewsbury, John, & Sons, Ltd. Littleton Street, Walsall, England. Unnumbered catalog (ca. World War I), Panhandle-Plains Historical Museum Research Center, Canyon.

Dodson Saddlery Co. Dallas, Tex. Catalog no. 23 (1916), Collection of Lloyd Mitchell, Gatesville, Tex.

Duhamel Company. Rapid City, S.D. Catalog no. 3 (1927), Panhandle-Plains Historical Museum Research Center, Canyon.

Ernst, Otto F., Inc. Sheridan, Wyo. Catalog no. 13 (1930), Panhandle-Plains Historical Museum Research Center, Canyon.

Evers, H. P. C., Saddlery. Brady, Tex. Unnumbered catalog (undated), Collection of Lloyd Mitchell, Gatesville, Tex.

Fiss, Doerr & Carroll Horse Co. New York. Harness Catalog (1906), Panhandle-Plains Historical Museum Research Center, Canyon.

Frazier, R. T. Saddlery. Pueblo, Colo. Catalog no. 24 (ca. 1924–25), Catalog no. 29 (undated), Estate of O. R. Huff, Fort Worth.

Fuqua, Jack. Amarillo, Tex. W. R. "Wallie"

Boone Catalog no. 3 (undated), Collection of Lloyd Mitchell, Gatesville, Tex.

Furstnow, Al., Saddlery Company. Miles City, Mont. Illustrated Catalog no. 31 (ca. 1930), Illustrated Catalog no. 32 (ca. 1931), Panhandle-Plains Historical Museum Research Center, Canyon.

Hamley & Co. Pendleton, Oreg. Catalog no. 2 (1912), unnumbered catalog (1919), Catalog no. 25 (1924), Catalog no. 26 (1925–26), Catalog no. 27 (1926–27), Catalog no. 29 (1929), Catalog no. 38 (1938), Catalog no. 39 (1939), Catalog no. 40 (1940), Catalog no. 50–51 (1950), Catalog no. 73 (1956), Panhandle-Plains Historical Museum Research Center, Canyon.

Haydens & Allen Co. Catalog no. 513 (1885), Collection of R. O. Lash, Belton, Tex.

Hess & Hopkins Leather Co. Rockford, Ill. Catalog no. 18 (Apr., 1947), Catalog no. 19 (Jan., 1949), Panhandle-Plains Historical Museum Research Center, Canyon.

Irick, J. T., Saddlery. Casper, Wyo. Unnumbered catalog (undated), Collection of Bob Taylor, Santa Fe.

Johnson, J. C. & Co. San Francisco, Calif. Unnumbered catalog (ca. 1896), Panhandle-Plains Historical Museum Research Center, Canyon.

Kauffman, H., & Sons. New York, N.Y. Unnumbered catalog (undated), Panhandle-Plains Historical Museum Research Center, Canyon.

Kelly, P. M., & Sons. El Paso, Tex. Catalog no. 64 (ca. 1960), Collection of Bob Taylor, Santa Fe.

Kelly Brothers. Dalhart, Tex. Catalog no. 17 (ca. 1920), Collection of Bob Taylor, Santa Fe.

Kelly Bros., Mfgs. El Paso, Tex. Catalog no. 20 (undated), Catalog no. 26 (undated). Panhandle-Plains Historical Museum Research Center, Canyon.

Keyston Bros. San Francisco, Calif. Catalog no. 78 (1941), Catalog no. 80 (1948), Catalog no. 102 (1973), Catalog no. 103 (1978), Catalog no. 104 (1978), Panhandle-Plains Historical Museum Research Center, Canyon.

Kingsville Lumber Company. Kingsville, Tex. Catalog no. 23 (1925), Panhandle-

Plains Historical Museum Research Center, Canyon.

Kyle Products, Inc. El Paso, Tex. Brochure (1974), Collection of Lyle and Jane Pattie, Aledo, Tex.

La Palestina. Mexico, D. F. Catalogo Ilustrado no. 40 (1932), Panhandle-Plains Historical Museum Research Center, Canyon.

Lee, E. C., Saddlery. Pierre, S. D. Catalog no. 20 (1927), Panhandle-Plains Historical Museum Research Center, Canyon.

Libertyville Saddle Shop, Inc. Libertyville, Ill. Unnumbered catalog (1981), Collection of Lyle and Jane Pattie, Aledo, Tex.

McChesney, J. R., Spurs and Bits. Gainesville, Tex. Unnumbered catalog (1906); Pauls Valley, Okla. Catalog no. 20 (undated), Collection of Lloyd Mitchell, Gatesville, Tex.

Main & Winchester. San Francisco, Calif. Catalog no. 11 (1897), Panhandle-Plains Historical Museum Research Center, Canyon.

Meanea, F. A., Cheyenne, Wyo. Unnumbered catalog (undated), Catalog no. 20 (1932), Panhandle-Plains Historical Museum Research Center, Canyon.

Miles City Saddlery Co. Miles City, Mont. Unnumbered catalog (192—), Collection of Jack Thomas, Fallbrook, Calif.; Catalog no. 29 (1927 or 1928), unnumbered catalog (1930), unnumbered catalog (1932), Panhandle-Plains Historical Museum Research Center, Canyon.

Miller, Blake. Cheyenne, Wyo. Unnumbered catalog (undated), Collection of Bob Taylor, Santa Fe; Catalog no. 12 (ca. 1922), Panhandle-Plains Historical Museum Research Center, Canyon.

Miller Harness Company, Inc. New York, N.Y. Catalog no. 55 (1940), Panhandle-Plains Historical Museum Research Center, Canyon; Catalog no. 104 (1972), Collection of Lyle and Jane Pattie, Aledo, Tex.

Miller Stockman. Denver, Colo. Spring/Summer Catalog (1972), Collection of Lyle and Jane Pattie, Aledo, Tex.

Morales, M. Los Angeles, Calif. Revised Price List no. 3 (undated); Portland, Ore. Catalog no. 5 (undated), Collection of Bob Taylor, Santa Fe.

Mueller, Fred, Saddle and Harness Co. Denver, Colo. Unnumbered catalog (1921), Collection of Lyle and Jane Pattie, Aledo, Tex.; Catalog no. 48 (1925), Panhandle-Plains Historical Museum Research Center, Canyon.

Myres, S. D., Saddle Co. El Paso, Tex. Unnumbered catalogs (1927–28, ca. 1939, ca. 1940, ca. 1950), Panhandle-Plains Historical Museum Research Center, Canyon.

Newberry's Hardware Co. Alliance, Neb. Unnumbered catalog (ca. 1921), Panhandle-Plains Historical Museum Research Center, Canyon.

Nobby Narness Co., Inc. Fort Worth. Unnumbered catalog (1945). Panhandle-Plains Historical Museum Research Center, Canyon.

Nocona Boot Co., Inc. Nocona, Tex. Catalog no. 8 (undated), Estate of O. R. Huff, Fort Worth; unnumbered catalog (1934), Panhandle-Plains Historical Museum Research Center, Canyon.

North & Judd Mfg. Co. New Britain, Conn. *Harness, Baggage, Belt and Blanket Hardware,* Catalog no. 82 (1909), Connecticut Historical Society Collection. *Anchor Brand Harness Hardware,* Catalog no. 83 (1914), Collection of Lloyd Mitchell, Gatesville, Tex. Catalog no. 87 (undated), Collection of Bob Taylor, Santa Fe. *Star Steel Silver,* Catalog no. 93 (1953), Panhandle-Plains Historical Museum Research Center, Canyon. *"Anchor Brand" Saddlery Hardware,* Price List no. 35 (1886–87), Collection of Ralph Emerson, Jr., Newington, Conn.

Olsen-Stelzer Boot & Saddlery Co. Henrietta, Tex. Unnumbered catalogs (1940, 1941), Panhandle-Plains Historical Museum Research Center, Canyon.

Olzer, Frank. Gillette, Wyo. Unnumbered catalog (ca. 1917), Collection of Bob Taylor, Santa Fe.

Overton's Bits & Spurs. Tyler, Tex. Brochure (ca. 1948), Panhandle-Plains Historical Museum Research Center, Canyon.

Ozark Leather Company, Inc. Waco, Tex. Catalog no. 71 (undated), unnumbered catalog (undated), Panhandle-Plains Historical Museum Research Center, Canyon.

Padgitt Bros. Co. Dallas, Tex. Catalog no. 83 (1917), Catalog no. 101 (1942), Panhandle-Plains Historical Museum Research Center, Canyon.

Phillips & Gutierrez. Cheyenne, Wyo. Reproduction of 1917 catalog by Reproductions West, Burbank, Calif., Collection of Lloyd Mitchell, Gatesville, Tex.

Porter, N., Co. Phoenix, Ariz. Catalog no. 32 (1941), Panhandle-Plains Historical Museum Research Center, Canyon.

Porter, N., Saddle & Harness Co. Phoenix, Ariz. Catalog no. 17 (1929–30), Catalog no. 18 (1930), Panhandle-Plains Historical Museum Research Center, Canyon.

Porter's. Phoenix, Ariz. Catalog no. 36 (1950), Panhandle-Plains Historical Museum Research Center, Canyon.

Porters Saddles and Saddle Accessories. Phoenix, Ariz. Catalog no. 38 (1950s), Panhandle-Plains Historical Museum Research Center, Canyon.

Rawhide Mfg., Inc. San Diego, Calif. Unnumbered catalogs (1975, 1977, 1977 Supplement), Panhandle-Plains Historical Museum Research Center, Canyon.

Renalde, Crockett & Kelly. Boulder, Colo. Catalog no. 578 (Jan. 1, 1979), Panhandle-Plains Historical Museum Research Center, Canyon.

Ricardo. Denver, Colo. Catalog no. 9 (1953); Victoria, Tex. Catalog no. 1070 (1977), Panhandle-Plains Historical Museum Research Center, Canyon.

Ruwart Manufacturing Co. Denver, Colo. Catalog no. 12 (1953), Panhandle-Plains Historical Museum Research Center, Canyon.

Ryon's Saddle & Ranch Supply. Fort Worth, Tex. Catalog no. 45 (Fall & Christmas, 1968), unnumbered catalog (Spring & Summer, 1975), Collection of Lyle and Jane Pattie, Aledo, Tex.

Schoellkopf, G. H., Saddlery Company. Dallas, Tex. Unnumbered catalog (undated), Collection of Bob Taylor, Santa Fe.

Schoellkopf Company. Dallas, Tex. Catalog no. 25 (1925), Panhandle-Plains Historical Museum Research Center, Canyon.

Schultz Brothers, Inc. North Manchester, Ind. Catalog no. 76 (1976), Panhandle-Plains Historical Museum Research Center, Canyon.

Sears, Roebuck & Company. Chicago, Ill. *Special Vehicle, Harness and Saddlery Catalog.* Unnumbered catalog (1897), Catalog no. 112 (1901), Panhandle-Plains Historical Museum Research Center, Canyon.

Shipley, Chas. P., Saddlery & Mercantile Co. Kansas City, Mo. Catalog no. 9 (ca. 1911), unnumbered catalog (1913), Catalog no. 16 (ca. 1917), Catalog no. 17 (1918), Catalog no. 18 (undated), Catalog no. 19 (1923), Catalog no. 23 (ca. 1928), Catalog no. 27 (1933), Cowboy Hall of Fame, Oklahoma City; unnumbered catalog (1935), Shipley Collection, Kansas City; unnumbered catalog (undated) picturing McChesney and Buermann spurs, Collection of Bob Taylor, Santa Fe.

Silver Tip Manufacturing. Chico, Calif. Unnumbered catalog (undated), Panhandle-Plains Historical Museum Research Center, Canyon.

Simco Leather Co., Inc. Chattanooga, Tenn. Unnumbered catalog (1971–72), Collection of Lyle and Jane Pattie, Aledo, Tex.; unnumbered catalog (1977–78), Panhandle-Plains Historical Museum Research Center, Canyon.

Sims, Ed, Spur Company. Uvalde, Tex. Unnumbered catalog (undated), Panhandle-Plains Historical Museum Research Center, Canyon.

Stockman Farmer Supply Co., Denver, Colo. Catalog no. 34 (1929), Panhandle-Plains Historical Museum Research Center, Canyon.

Texas Tanning & Manufacturing Co. Yoakum, Tex. Catalog no. 39 (1930s), Panhandle-Plains Historical Museum Research Center, Canyon.

TexTan of Yoakum. Yoakum, Tex. Catalog no. 4 (1951), Catalog no. 66 (1957), Catalog no. 67 (1958), Catalog no. 70 (1960), Panhandle-Plains Historical Museum Research Center, Canyon.

Veach Saddlery Company. Trenton, Mo. Catalog no. 3 (ca. 1949), Panhandle-Plains Historical Museum Research Center, Canyon.

Victor Leather Goods. Pasadena, Calif. Catalog no. 71 (undated); Paramount, Calif. Catalog no. 76 (undated), Panhandle-Plains Historical Museum Research Center, Canyon.

Visalia Stock Saddle Co. San Francisco, Calif. Catalog no. 21C (1924), Catalog no. 31 (ca. 1935), unnumbered catalog (1950), Catalog no. 35 (1952), Panhandle-Plains Historical Museum Research Center, Canyon; Grass Valley, Calif. Unnumbered catalog (1970), Collection of Lyle and Jane Pattie, Aledo, Tex.; Catalog no. 101 (July, 1971), Panhandle-Plains Historical Museum Research Center, Canyon.

Vogt Western Silver, Ltd. Turlock, Calif. Unnumbered catalog (1976), Panhandle-Plains Historical Museum Research Center, Canyon.

Western Ranchman Outfitters. Cheyenne, Wyo. Catalog no. 34 (Spring & Summer, 1955), Panhandle-Plains Historical Museum Research Center, Canyon.

Western Saddle Manufacturing Co. Denver, Colo. Catalog no. 30 (1926), Catalog no. 49 (ca. 1945), Panhandle-Plains Historical Museum Research Center, Canyon.

White & Davis. Pueblo, Colo. Catalog no. 19 (1922), Panhandle-Plains Historical Museum Research Center, Canyon.

Wyeth Hardware & Manufacturing Co. St. Joseph, Mo. Catalog no. 196 (1930s), Panhandle-Plains Historical Museum Research Center, Canyon.

Interviews and Correspondence

Anderson, Ray. Weatherford, Tex. Apr. 14, 1989.

Anglin, Robert, and Belva Anglin. Safford, Ariz. Apr. 15, 1983.

Anglin, Mary Causey. Safford, Ariz. Apr. 15, 1983.

Baker, France, to author. Lubbock, Tex. Feb. 7 and Oct. 16, 1974.

Baker, Jack R. Sonora, Tex. Apr. 2, 1988.

Baker, Jack R., to author. Sonora, Tex. Apr. 23, 1988.

Bass, J. O., Jr. Plainview, Tex. (telephone interviews). June 1, 1978; Feb. 2, 1988.

Bayers, Adolph R. Truscott, Tex. Mar. 6, 1972.

Bayers, Fannie Louis, to author. Truscott, Tex. Dec. 14, 1982; Feb. 8, 1988.

Blanchard, Edward R. Yucca, Ariz. June 1, 1973.

Blanchard, Mrs. Arthur H., to author. Cherry Valley, Calif. May 21, 1978.

Boone, Bob. San Diego, Calif. May 28, 1973.

Boone, Bob, to author. San Diego, Calif. Jan. 17, 1973.

Boone, Dee. Henryetta, Okla. May 1, 1973.

Boone, Pate. Christoval, Tex. Feb. 4, 1975.

Boone, Pate, to author. Christoval, Tex. Mar. 15, 1979.

Bowman, Joe. Houston, Tex. Apr. 20, 1983.

Browning, Lewis W., to author. Angleton, Tex. Mar. 3 and July 14, 1989.

Buntyn, Juanita. Sonora, Tex. Dec. 10, 1983.

Castello, Jeannine, (Tom Green County Library) to author. San Angelo, Tex. Jan. 27, 1983.

Castro, Virgie. Pauls Valley, Okla. May 12, 1983.

Crockett, Hazel A. Boulder, Colo. May 16, 1975.

Crockett, Hazel A., to author. Boulder, Colo. Mar. 14, May 20, and Sept. 13, 1975; Feb. 12, 1976.

Davidson, Duval. Fort Worth, Tex. Oct. 8, 1973.

Doyle, Mona Buermann. Brooklyn, N.Y. (telephone interview). Nov. 12, 1983.

Emerson, Ralph L., Jr. Newington, Conn. (telephone interviews). Nov. 11, 1983; Jan. 7, 1984; Aug. 12, 1989.

Emerson, Ralph L., to author. Newington, Conn. Dec. 8, 1986.

Fish, Frances. Menard, Tex. (telephone interview). Aug. 17, 1977.

Fish, Frances, to author. Menard, Tex. Sept. 1, 1977.

Foster, Dean, (McCurtain County Historical Society) to author. Idabel, Okla. May 19, 1983.

Gabriella, Al. Boulder, Colo. May 6, 1975.

Gayler, Billie Sue (Swisher County Museum). Tulia, Tex. (telephone interview). Feb. 2, 1988.

Gollaher, Blanch Boone. San Diego, Calif. May 28, 1973.

Gollaher, Blanch Boone, to author. San Diego, Calif. Mar. 5, 1973.

Grimmett, Adrienne, (Pauls Valley City Library) to author. Pauls Valley, Okla. Jan. 27, 1983.

Haas, Gloria, (Chamber of Commerce) to author. Coleman, Tex. Feb. 15, 1983.

Hanbury, Dessie, (Dallam-Hartley Historical Association). Dalhart, Tex. (telephone interview). July 1, 1983.

Hanbury, Dessie, (Dallam-Hartley Historical Association) to author. Dalhart, Tex. July 8, 1983.

Hays, A. P., (West Galleries, Inc.) to Marcia Preston (*Persimmon Hill* magazine). Scottsdale, Ariz. July 26, 1988.

Hildebrand, W. W., to author. Glendale, Calif. Mar. 17, 1976.

Hubbard, Lee, (Carlsbad City Museum). Carlsbad, N.Mex. June 15, 1988; July 6, 1989.

Huber, Dwight, Canyon, Tex. Apr. 28, 1983.

Huff, O. R. Fort Worth, Tex. Aug. 2 and Aug. 12, 1972.

Justin, Enid, (Nocona Boot Company). Nocona, Tex. (telephone interview). May 15, 1978.

Kelly, Hettie Vititoe. El Paso, Tex. Aug. 15, 1969.

Kelly, Hettie, to author. El Paso, Tex. Letters from May 14, 1973 to July 9, 1983.

Kelly, Jack, to author. Oceanside, Calif. May 31, 1975; Feb. 19, 1987.

Kelly, Pascal M. Oceanside, Calif. Aug. 1, Sept. 13, Dec. 1, 1972; June 28, 1973.

Kelly, Pascal M., to author. Oceanside, Calif. tape recordings: May 19 and Oct. 1, 1975; Jan. 1, May 27, June 24, Oct. 24, Dec. 3, and Dec. 11, 1974; May 19, 1975.

Lehne, Louie. Menard, Tex. (telephone interview). Dec. 10, 1983.

Lindley, Jerry. Weatherford, Tex. May 2, 1984; Sept. 20, 1988.

McCain, Diana, (Conn. Historical Society) to author. Hartford, Conn. Apr. 4, and May 22, 1978; Mar. 6, 1979.

McChesney, Edna. Pauls Valley, Okla. May 12, 1983.

McChesney, Mrs. Robert. Ardmore, Okla. (telephone interview). May 15, 1978.

McPherson, Clinton. Valley View, Tex. Oct. 10, 1983.

McPherson, Kirby. Santa Fe. N.Mex. Nov. 20, 1982.

Marks, Emil. Barker, Tex. Apr. 15, 1969.

Miller, C. E. Mason, Tex. Feb. 12, 1972.

Mitchell, Lloyd. Gatesville, Tex. Oct. 7, 1969; Aug. 12, 1974.

Mitchell, Lloyd, to author. Gatesville, Tex. July 5 and Aug. 8, 1974; Aug. 2, 1984.

Moore, Glynard, (Moore Spurs). Matador, Tex. Mar. 15, 1989.

Moore, Glynard, to author. Matador, Tex. Mar. 20 and Apr. 13, 1989.

Muter, Shirley. Middletown, Conn. (telephone interview). Nov. 11, 1983.

Panell, Jewell. Pauls Valley, Okla. May 12, 1983.

Pliska, Mary Beth. Midland, Tex. (telephone interview). Feb. 19, 1975.

Potts, Marisue, (Motley Co. Historical Commission) to author. June 4 and June 16, 1989.

Price, B. Byron, (Panhandle-Plains Historical Museum) to author. Canyon, Tex. Jan. 31, 1983.

Rattenbury, Richard, (National Cowboy Hall of Fame and Western Heritage Center) to author. Oklahoma City, Okla., June 16, and Oct. 8, 1988.

Reagan, Tom. Beeville, Tex. July 28, 1983.

Schad, Paul J. Gainesville, Tex. (telephone interview). Nov. 5, 1983.

Schad, Paul J., to author. Gatesville, Tex. Nov. 7, 1983.

Shook, Robert, (Victoria College). Victoria, Tex. (telephone interview). Oct. 10, 1978.

Shook, Robert, to author. Victoria, Tex. Oct. 12, 1977.

Sims, Ed. Uvalde, Tex. Oct. 1, 1975.

Sparks, Van. Pauls Valley, Okla. (telephone interview). May 12, 1983.

Spencer, Dick, (*Western Horseman* magazine) to author. Colorado Springs, Colo. Dec. 9, 1972.

Spiller, Wayne, to author. Voca, Tex. Oct. 12, 1983.

Steffen, Randy. Lingleville, Tex. Mar. 11, 1976.

Taylor, Bob. Houston, Tex. Mar. 16 and Apr. 20, 1983.

Taylor, Bob, to author. Houston, Tex. Mar. 30, 1983; Santa Fe, N.Mex. Aug. 23, 1988.

Terry, Ralph, to author. Coleman, Tex. Dec. 15, 1983.

Thomas, Jack. Fallbrook, Calif. June 29, 1973; May 27, 1975.

Thomas, Jack, to author. Fallbrook, Calif.

May 27, 1975; Mar. 19 and Apr. 4, 1988.

Treadwell, John. Fort McKavett, Tex. (telephone interview). Dec. 10, 1983.

Trimble, L. E. Eden, Tex. Feb. 2, 1974.

Wall, Elva, to author. Pauls Valley, Okla. June 1, 1983.

Wedderburn, Maizy L., (Newark Public Library) to author. Newark, N.J. May 3, May 22, and May 30, 1984.

Wheat, Jim. Mentone, Tex. Oct. 3, 1983.

Wheless, Lynell. Menard, Tex. Apr. 2, 1988.

Willard, Joe. Pauls Valley, Okla. May 12, 1983.

Wilson, John. Pyote, Tex. Oct. 3, 1988.

Woodward, Arthur. Patagonia, Ariz. Oct. 15, 1973.

Index

(NOTE: Numbers in **boldface** refer to illustrations on that page.)

Index